# EMPOWERMENT OF RURAL INDIAN WOMEN

# EMPOWERMENT OF RURAL INDIAN WOMEN
## Study of Uttarakhand

Dr. Mrs. Zainab Rahman

Publications
KALPAZ PUBLICATIONS
DELHI-110052

Empowerment of Rural Indian Women

ISBN : 81-7835-605-8



Published in 2007 in India by
Kalpaz Publications
C-30, Satyawati Nagar, Delhi-110052
E-mail : Kalpaz@hotmail. com

*Laser Typesetting at* : Master Computers, Delhi
*Printed at* : Salasar Imaging System, Delhi

## *Dedication*

***Dedicated to the courageous and hardworking women of Uttarakhand***

# Contents

# Map of the Hill State Uttarakhand

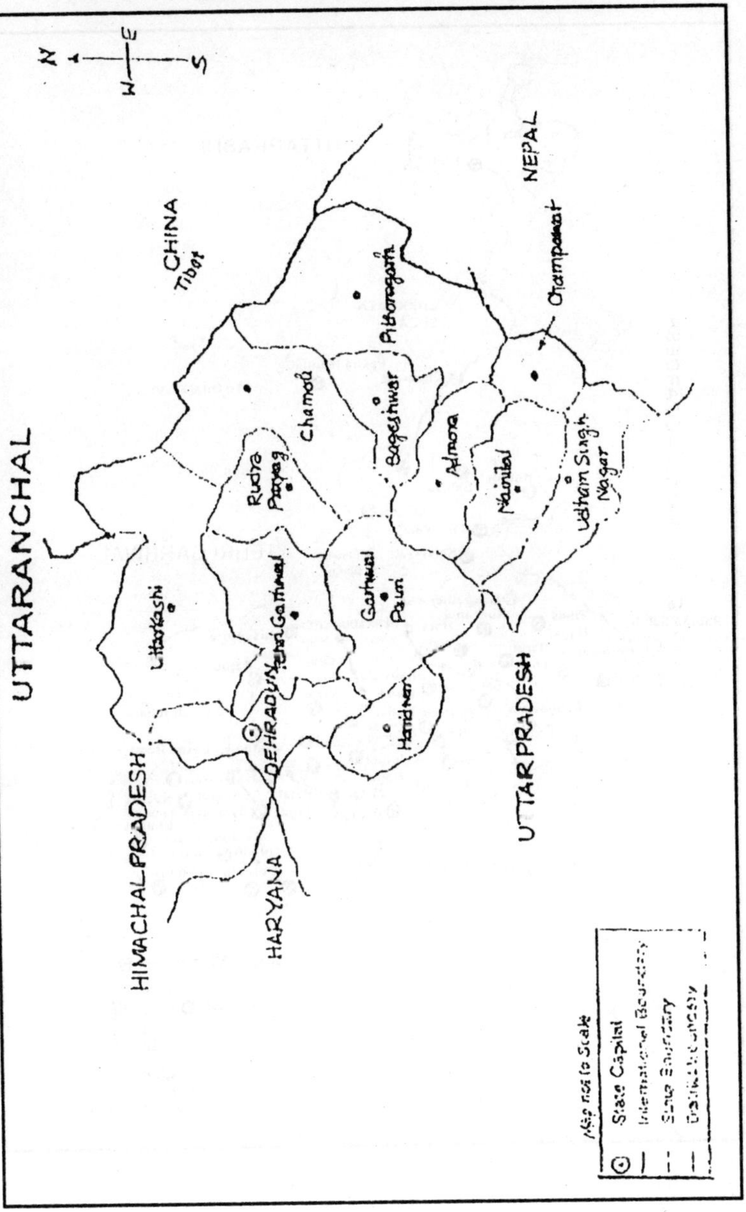

# Map of Dehradun District

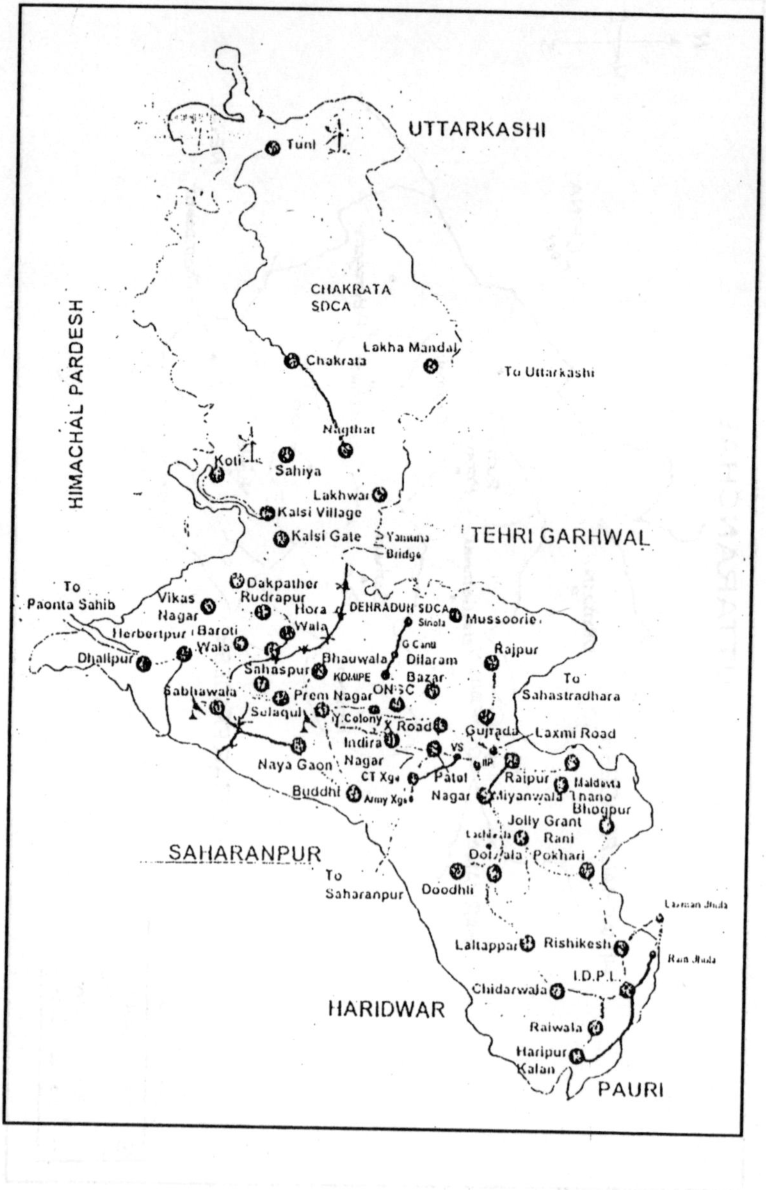

**Radha Raturi, IAS**
Secretary

उत्तरा खण्ड शासन

**Government of Uttarakhand**
**Women Empowerment & Child Development Department**

# Foreword

Women's empowerment is not an issue related to "women" alone, it is an issue of creating a more civilized society, where every human being can live a life of fulfillment and dignity. All over the world, women work more than men, but their domestic work is not recognized, because it is generally not quantified in monetary terms.

Our constitution has given equal rights to men and women, but legal equality has not translated into economic empowerment and gender justice. This book by Dr. Mrs. Zainab Rahman is a commendable effort to evaluate the level of empowerment of rural women in Uttarakhand. It is based on a study of ten villages in two development blocks of Dehradun district. This book will be helpful for Government departments, NGOs and social activists who are working on the issue of empowering women and helping them to shape their own destiny.

**Radha Raturi**

# Preface

Empowerment of women is a comparatively new concept which has gained importance in the last decade in our national planning for improving the status of women. The year 2001 was celebrated as the Women's Empowerment Year, in India A comprehensive strategy for women's empowerment has been outlined in the Ninth and Tenth Five Year Plans and various schemes have been implemented for this purpose. It is generally felt that in our patriarchal society, women are powerless and they are treated as subordinates. If they are empowered they will be able to achieve gender equality. Empowerment is a multi faceted word. It includes elements like freedom of choice and decision making, freedom to shape one's own destiny and economic freedom. Towards this end the government has started many projects with the express purpose of providing employment, entrepreneurship and political participation to women. There has been some progress in improving women's condition both economically and politically in rural as well as urban areas but gender parity is yet a distant dream. The social set up in our town and villages is such that women continue to be exploited and treated as inferior to men. There has to be a change in attitudes and behaviour to achieve gender equality and to make the various schemes really successful. Increasing the general awareness of people and sensitizing them towards gender justice are ways of bringing about positive change in thinking. This is being done by the media and by voluntary organizations quite effectively. It is creditable that there is noticeable change even in villages. The rural women are increasingly becoming aware of their rights and are making efforts to achieve them. They are seriously involved in improving their socio economic status by utilizing all the opportunities available to them. These include capacity building activities, political participation, cooperative efforts in the form of SHGs and Mahila Mangal Dals and entrepreneurship.

This book is a modified version of the Report prepared for a UGC Minor Project entitled 'Empowerment of Rural Indian Women'. It presents the details of the study made in ten villages of Garhwal region as well as provides information about the level of empowerment and the general condition of rural women in the entire state of Uttarakhand with a separate chapter on the empowerment level of rural women in Kumaon region. The four main criteria selected to measure the level of empowerment of rural women in this book are : economic independence, political participation, decision making power and access to basic facilities, since all these are essential elements of empowerment. Empowerment has been variously defined as the process by which the powerless gain greater control over the circumstances of their lives. It includes both control over resources and over ideology. [Presser and Sen 2000] Brinda Karat writes, the substance of women's empowerment can be measured by how far women have advanced in the spheres of economic independence and equality, in political assertion, in being able to live a violence free life and in being able to break social and cultural barriers which keep women in subordinate positions. Thus empowerment means control over various aspects of one's life. One has to understand that this control has to be achieved with one's own efforts and determination. No one can empower an unwilling person, nor can empowerment be handed out. It has to be earned.

In our country women have shown that when ever need arises they face challenges and come out successful. They have the potential to achieve success. What is required is motivation and awareness. Once offered the opportunity, women have utilized it to make progress. Today, many rural women have benefited through formation of Self Help Groups and through capacity building programmes and have become economically self reliant. Similarly in the past decade rural women have increasingly availed of the opportunity of fighting the local elections from reserved seats and becoming Panchayat members. This book shows how the women of Uttarakhand have taken part in socio-political and environmental movements and achieved their goals. In fact many times they have spearheaded these movements. The study also shows that some respondents have leadership qualities and have worked for welfare of their village and womenfolk.

Today rural women are making fast progress and becoming more assertive. They are not only improving their own lives but are making every effort to educate their daughters and give them the freedom which they did not receive themselves. This points to a better future for women in villages. In the next generation, the women will be more empowered. Of course access to basic facilities and gender parity are not yet very satisfactory, but steps in the right direction are being taken. More effort is required to increase awareness and create gender sensitivity among men, so that they support the women's cause.

This book is an attempt to highlight the achievements of the rural women of Uttarakhand and also to bring to the notice of planners and policy makers the different problems and hindrances faced by these women in achieving their goals and empowering themselves. It also provides information about the various facilities and schemes that are available to rural women in the state, both through government agencies and also through voluntary organizations. If this book is of help to either women or planners in any way the main purpose of writing it would be served and the author would feel highly satisfied.

**Dr Zainab Rahman**
Reader. Deptt. of Sociology
MKP PG College, Dehradun

# Acknowledgements

This book is a modified version of a Project Report entitled "Empowerment of Rural Indian Women". The project was funded by the University Grants Commission. I acknowledge with thanks this grant from the UGC. My thanks are also due to Mr. Pati Ram, Under Secretary UGC, for taking a personal interest in my work and providing help and guidance when ever I asked for it.

I am extremely thankful to Smt. Radha Raturi, Secretary, Women Empowerment and Child Development Department, Govt. of Uttarakhand, for writing an inspiring foreword to my book. I am very grateful to my College Principals, Smt. J Bhandari, who encouraged me to apply for the UGC grant, Smt. Shanta Tankha who helped and encouraged me during the two years of my field work and report writing and Dr. Indu Singh, always an inspiring senior colleague, who forwarded my Final Report as the new Principal.

I have received help and guidance from various seniors, colleagues and friends in my field work and writing of the report. I express my gratitude to all of them. Above all I am extremely thankful to all my respondents for their unfailing cooperation. I have been helped in data collection, classification and tabulation work by my research students,

Shabnam, Poornima and Archana. I owe thanks to them too. I hope they too have learnt a lot by working on this project. I also thank the members of the College Office Staff who have helped in various ways with the official work. Last but not least I am thankful to my family members for their moral support and help.

Empowerment of women is an issue very close to my heart, therefore I have really enjoyed working on this project and I hope it will prove to be of some value to planners and social workers as well as to students of social sciences. That would be a great reward to me for my hard work.

**Dr. Zainab Rahman**

# 1

# Introduction

Women have always worked side by side with men in all societies and contributed equally, if not more, to the economy, family welfare, community life and human progress in general but they have always been given a subordinate position and subjugated by men both in the name of religion and social institutions. The status of women in different societies at different times has varied to some extent due to prevailing conditions, but it has always been subordinate to that of man. In fact research and studies by women scholars all over the world are proving that a majority of women enjoyed a better status in earlier times than they do now in modern times when most civilized societies acknowledge that women should be given equal status to men and many countries grant equality legally. This is quite a paradox. Modern development, while it has improved living standards in general and enabled man to conquer the world, has not benefited women much. In fact it has been detrimental to their social and economic position in society. because it is based on a Western, patriarchal scientific paradigm.

### Status of Women

"Women have been the subordinate gender in most of the history that we know and they are still the second sex in all the countries, without exception. There are different ways in which they have been subordinated. Women have had less control over resources, including their own bodies, in all societies and that continues to be so everywhere. All phenomena commonly associated with global interactions such as trade, nationalism, state building and so on, have had contradictory influences on women's lives through out history."[1] For instance during the industrial revolution in England while men earned more money and freedom from feudal system, women lost many of their previous professions, like spinning. Similarly in India industrialization destroyed cottage industries which were the main source of women's employment. Esther Boserup has documented how women's impoverishment increased during colonial rule. She writes, those rulers who had already subjugated their women as deskilled and de-intellectualised appendages, disfavoured the women of the colonies on matters of access to land, technology and employment. Thus women were displaced from productive activity by the expansion of development because these projects destroyed the natural resource base for the production of sustenance.[2]

Women have the primary role of homemakers in all societies since time immemorial, but in primitive societies they contributed a lot to the economy as well as community life, whereas in modern times, with the exception of a small number of urban educated women, the general masses of women have been marginalised in economy and community activities. There are many reasons for this. Today specialization has increased and technical skills are essential for meaningful contribution to the economy, which the ordinary women lack. The earlier economic pursuits of women, namely cottage industries have been displaced. Earlier women's contribution to family occupation was valued just like that of men, but today unpaid labour is not recognized.

Women have been confined to housework, which although it is extremely important for humanity, is not even considered as 'work' because it does not fetch money. Modern development and capitalism go hand in hand, and all over the world, specially in the third world countries, these processes are undermining the role and status of women. Feminism is an effort to re-establish the ancient status of women which was more satisfactory.

## Women in India

When India became independent the Govt. opted for national planning with the aim of balanced development and social justice. Our Constitution gave equal rights to all citizens regardless of religion, caste creed or sex. Thus women achieved legal equality and the right to vote and other rights same as men. At first the women's organizations and the Govt. were under the impression that now women will automatically make good progress due to these equal rights. Besides in the First five year Plan the Govt outlined the philosophy to "promote the welfare of women" so that they can play their legitimate role in the family and community. For this purpose Central Social Welfare Board was set up in 1953 to promote voluntary organizations at various levels specially at the grassroots; to take up welfare activities for women. This welfare approach continued for nearly two decades.[3] In 1975 when the CSWI published its report, Towards Equality, it became clear that these measures had not proved very successful in improving the lot of women and the truth was that most women were facing exploitation and discrimination in all most all spheres and with the exception of a small number of urban middle class women, none had made progress and general conditions were unsatisfactory. This led to a concern for women's development and for the first time women were recognized as participants and not beneficiaries in the process of development. This shift in approach from "welfare" to "development" was introduced in the Sixth Five Year Plan (1980-1985) and for this it is considered a milestone in planning for women's development In this Plan a chapter on Women and Development was included at the instigation of women's organisations. The Plan adopted a multi-disciplinary approach with a special thrust on the three core sectors of health, education and employment. Accordingly, priority was given to implementation of programmes for women under agriculture and allied activities. In later plans too women's development programmes were given importance; but feminists continued to assert that modern development has not really benefited women mainly because their participation in development was enforced and asymmetrical so much so that they bore the brunt but were excluded from its benefits. This fact was corroborated by UN findings too when its specialists analysed the responses of member nations to the UN Questionnaire on progress made during Women's Decade. They noted that development has not always benefited women, instead it could lead to further marginalisation of women. Feminists therefore suggest alternative strategies, like sustainable development which would benefit women too.

Notwithstanding the detrimental effect of modern development on masses of Indian women, the standard of living has in general improved all over the country, both in cities and villages. Spread of education and mass media has improved the general awareness of all. Better health facilities are also available, to lesser or greater extent, both in urban and rural areas. Literacy rates have improved. Of course much needs to be done still, mainly in the villages, where basic facilities are yet not available to all. Remote villages are still very backward. The ninth and tenth plans laid stress on providing minimum essential facilities to all which include clean drinking water, primary health care, electricity and roads. Indian villages face numerous problems Joel SGR Bose writes in detail about the rural people and their problems. He says 50 years after independence nearly 600 million people living in about 6 lakh villages are generally backward both economically and educationally, oppressed socially, suppressed culturally and exploited politically as well as deprived of access to basic facilities. The major rural problems are poverty, casteism, women's exploitation, unemployment, unremunerative agriculture, lack of basic amenities and denial of information.[4] The Government policies too, are not very beneficial to the rural poor. In such a scenario, rural women are all the more oppressed, since in our traditional society restrictions of various kinds are placed on women, specially in the villages. Inspite of doing a lot of hard work, rural women have a very low status and are dependent on men. Narsimhan writes that poor women from Scheduled. Castes and Tribes, in the villages carry a triple handicap : firstly because they are women, secondly because they are rural and thirdly because they are of low caste.[5] It is true that poor men also suffer but women suffer more because they are exploited both by their own men and men of higher castes and classes Women fare worse than men in terms of all sets of development indices Women's access to and ownership of resources is less than that enjoyed by men. Just like the gender gap in development there is also a big gap in rural and urban development, hence rural women have more problems and less facilities as compared to urban women. Finally the scheduled castes and tribes are the marginalized groups in villages who are the poorest of the poor and suffer from a host of social and cultural disabilities even today.

## Women and Development

Let us now see what all has happened in the last two decades in our country to improve the lot of women. The

Government of India introduced the New Economic Policy at the beginning of the 90s which ushered in an era of liberalization, privatization and finally globalization. All these have proved beneficial to the urban rich and harmful to the rural poor, including both men and women. On the other hand the Government is also committed to the women's cause and hence has been introducing schemes for women's equality and empowerment in the five year plans. In the Ninth Plan two significant changes were made in the conceptual strategy for planning for women. First, "Empowerment of women" became one of the nine primary objectives of the plan. The approach of the Plan was to create an enabling environment for women to freely exercise their rights as equal partners with men. Second, the Plan attempted the convergence of existing services, resources, infrastructure and man power available in both women–specific and women-related sectors. It directed the Centre and States to ensure the flow of ear marked funds for women through an effective mechanism to empower women. The year 2001 was declared Women's Empowerment Year and the National Policy for the Empowerment of Women was adopted. The Policy aims at :

- the advancement, development and empowerment of women in all spheres of life
- introduction of more responsive judicial legal systems that are sensitive to women's needs
- ensuring women's equality in power sharing and active participation in decision making
- mainstreaming a gender perspective in the development process
- comprehensive economic and social empowerment of women.

- The Ninth Plan made a brilliant situational analysis of women in India but it refrained from making any commitment for achieving any specific goal or target. Hence it was considered that the Tenth Five Year Plan should break a new ground by fixing certain quantitative targets for empowerment of women and outline a strategy for achieving the same. This change in approach is justified because the status of women in India, as reflected in Gender Development Index, continues to be abysmally poor. And an improvement in women's status will also improve various other sectors like health, literacy and economy. A strategy to achieve the targets will have to be worked out in consultation with all other sectoral departments/Ministries, and adequate resources should be allotted and utilized properly. Monitorable targets set by the Tenth Plan include the following :

  — Reduce gender gaps in literacy and wage rates by atleast 50% by 2007

  — Reduce maternal mortality rate to 2 per 1000 live births by 2007 and to 1 by 2012

  — Reduce infant mortality rate to 45 per 1000 live births by 2007 and to 28 by 2012

  — Reduce decadal rate of population growth between 2001 and 2011 to 16.2%

  — Increase literacy rates to 75% by 2007

  — Reduce poverty ratio by 5% by 2007 and by 15% by 2012

  — Provide sustained access to potable water to all villages by 2007

— Provide gainful and high quality employment to the addition to labour force over the Tenth Plan period.

Empowerment of women is one of the central concerns of the Tenth Plan (2002-2007) which spells out a three–pronged strategy for it :

- **Social Empowerment** : create an enabling environment for development of women and give them easy and equal access to all the basic minimum services so that they can realize their full potential.

- **Economic Empowerment** : ensure provision of training, employment and income generation activities to make women economically self-reliant.

- **Gender Justice** : eliminate all forms of gender discrimination so that women are able to enjoy equal rights not only in theory but also in practice.

In the last ten years many steps have been taken by the Government and other agencies to empower women. An important measure was the reservation of 33% seats for women in Panchayat and local bodies' elections. Efforts towards gender sensitization of a traditionally male dominated society have been intensified. In this respect the gender sensitization of law enforcement agencies including police and judiciary, through periodic training is worth mentioning.[6] Inspite of all these efforts, much remains to be done to achieve gender equality, both in urban and rural areas. Awareness has definitely increased among all women and they are striving to achieve their rights, thanks to the commendable work done by NGOs and women's organizations. Still only a small number of women, mostly in urban areas, has achieved equality, in professions and public life. Equality in family life is yet to be achieved in our male dominated society. It is well known that rural women are less educated and less aware of their rights than urban women, in general. Hence their status is comparatively lower although they work the most. Rural women have always been producers of food and sustainers of the family.

Women have traditionally wanted to increase the productivity of food crop and domestic food production, which remain largely within the feminine domain. In the modern global scenario, a culture of cash crop production, largely controlled by the organised sector is being promoted. This has led to a change in land ownership from community to large private holdings or Govt. ownership. Distribution of resources and mechanization have gone against the interest of rural women. Green revolution technologies have also benefited men more than women.

With this background, it is clear that today rural women are suffering in many ways due to modern development strategies and specially more due to recent trends of globalization. Women are special victims of the new development processes like globalisation, liberalization and privatization. They need to be encouraged to empower themselves so that they are able to utilize their full potential in improving their lot and contributing to welfare of society.

**Empowerment of Women**

It is necessary at this stage to explain the term 'Empowerment' as it has been understood by leading feminists and activists. Noted feminist and political activist Brinda Karat writes, 'The substance of women's empowerment can be measured by how far women have advanced in the spheres of economic independence and equality, in political assertion, in being able to live a violence free life and in being able to break social and cultural barriers which keep women in subordinate positions.' Srilatha Batliwala gives a widely quoted definition of women's empowerment (Presser and Sen 2000) as follows : Empowerment is the process by which the powerless gain greater control over the circumstances of their lives. It includes both control over resources (physical, human, intellectual, financial) and over ideology (beliefs, values and attitudes) Elaborating on this she further writes.' It means not only greater extrinsic control, but also a growing intrinsic capacity–greater self-confidence and an inner transformation of one's consciousness that enables one to overcome external barriers to accessing resources or changing traditional ideology. Genuine empowerment includes both these aspects. 'Zainab Rahman writes, ' Empowerment is not a commodity that can be handed over to women. Power is an analytical category which denotes strength or control. It is something that has to develop from within. One cannot empower women if they are unwilling or if they are not equipped for it. Empowerment comes to women when they strive hard for it'. (Rahman 2005) She further writes, 'Empowerment aims at making women self-reliant and self confident so that they feel secure and are in a position to take their own decisions'

Narasimhan writes that money is not the main problem in the context of women's empowerment but apathy, fear, ignorance and vulnerability as women within patriarchal patterns of behaviour are the main problems. Awareness generation and psychological motivation are important means by which women can overcome their fears and inhibitions and come forward to empower themselves.

There are various factors or agents that can enhance the process of empowerment. The major ones are education, cooperative and organized efforts by women to improve their lot, economic independence and participation in decision making processes both at home and in the community at various levels of political activity. In India we have very good examples of all these agents at work and their positive contribution to women's empowerment. These will be discussed in detail in the forthcoming chapters.

**Present Study**

The present study focuses on the empowerment of rural women in ten villages in Dehradun district in Uttarakhand. The researcher selected a sample of 200 respondents by purposive stratified sampling technique and did her field work in the second half of the year 2005. Next she conducted some in depth interviews in all the villages over a period of six months to collect more information and to clear some doubts and ambiguities that had arisen while categorizing and tabulating the data. A detailed description of the objectives, methodology and universe is given in the next chapter.

This is a micro study of women's empowerment in rural setup and aims to provide first hand information about rural women's condition culled through intimate dialogue with them. The researcher hopes that this study will encourage further studies in this direction in other hilly areas so that women's condition in different areas may be compared and the shortcomings as well as positive aspects highlighted. Such information can be of immense help to the planning authorities and local NGOs who are involved with women's development. It will also add to the knowledge of indigenous communities in women's studies.

**Book Review**

There is a lot of literature about rural women and development programs for them. Recently many studies have been made regarding empowerment of rural women and related aspects like political participation, economic emancipation, literacy, legal literacy, health care and role of women in village level politics as well as environmental conservation and various types of social movements. I have reviewed a number of books and journals which have a bearing on the present project in one way or the other. I will now discuss some of the literature that I have reviewed.

In her book RURAL WOMEN, Management in farm and home, (1987), A. Laxmi Devi has presented her empirical study and its findings related to role performance of rural women in farm and home living in Krishna District of Andhra Pradesh. The main finding of the study was that rural women play an important role in rural economy. Their role performance determines to a great extent the success or failure of several production programmes at village level which influence rural economy. It was found that many variables like education, leadership qualities, caste, family size, liberal outlook, family norms, motivation and knowledge of home and farm management influence role performance. Depending on these influences women were categorized as high, average and poor performers by the researcher and she made various suggestions to improve the performance of average and poor performers. Her other findings were as follows :

Rural women work hard but earn less and have little or no access to technology or training. They are not aware of their rights or privileges. They need to be trained and organised, so that they may improve their lot. She says when women contribute to income they tend to participate in decision making process of the family.

Cultural barriers and taboos are major hindrances to middle and upper class rural women to take part in certain farm operations. Only poor rural women, out of economic hardships participate in farm operations as agricultural labourers and face many problems like harsh working condition, long hours, low wages, job insecurity, health problems and hazards. She concludes that the Government should try to improve conditions for rural women so that they lead more comfortable lives and also contribute more to rural welfare.

In the book, Panchayati Raj and Empowerment of Women (2004) AK Sinha gives a detailed account of the empowerment of women in villages in Haryana State, based on his field work. He gives detailed information of Panchayati Raj institutions and the history of gram panchayats. He says that in the State of Haryana women Panchs and Sarpanchs participate actively, to greater and lesser extent in all important functions of the Panchayat like social, economic, educational, political, public work and civic amenities, agriculture, trade and commerce, sanitation and medical relief and judicial work. Some factors that affect the role performance of Sarpanchs were : The Sarpanch who is free from the household chores can perform better than the Sarpanch who has to do housework and take care of children. Education was not the sole factor to make a woman Sarpanch assertive, as even little educated Sarpanchs were assertive due to their knowledge of village problems and needs. Those who were not exposed to outside world found it difficult to interact with Government officials. He writes that after 73rd amendment women and specially Scheduled caste women have started taking part in village level politics in greater numbers and this is a positive trend as women get a chance to participate in decision-making and it serves as a training ground for democracy and political education.

In the book, NGOs and Rural Development, (2003) the author Joel S. G. R Bhose gives detailed account of different type of NGOs working in our country and focuses on those which are helping the rural poor by their voluntary work. He says that while there are many schemes for rural development, they cannot be really effective in solving the problems of rural poor unless some social workers get involved with the implementation of the scheme in a truly dedicated way. He says that members of NGOs all over the country carry out their work with a humanitarian concern and professional wisdom for the betterment and sustainable development of the poor communities with the involvement of the people themselves. The book explains the term development in great detail giving an account of development indicators which show the level of development of a particular community. It also explains rural development and sustainable development and the role of NGOs in achieving all this. Development refers to a process of continuous progress unyoking the people from the stages of dependency towards self reliance, assuring equitable distribution of opportunities and resources and ensuring socio-economic justice and harmony among all sections of the society. Sustainable development is balanced and continued development in which regenerative level of the system is maintained. There are three main approaches to sustainability : economic, socio-cultural and environmental. Rural development is a strategy designed to improve the economic and social life of a specific group of people–the rural poor. Since Independence rural development has been given top priority in Indian planning. Presently a variety of rural development programmes are being implemented by the government NGOs play an important role in rural development by their interventions. They have achieved what the government and corporate sector did not, because they are concerned with the people and peoples' development is their goal. The book describes the various functions of the NGOs in separate chapters. Some of them are : reaching out to the people of the lowest stratum, creating all types of awareness among them, educating them, giving them training, capacity building, organizing self help groups, helping with banking and community programmes etc. The book also provides valuable information on people's participation in rural development, importance of empowering rural people and the need for advocacy to influence government policies in favour of the poor. The author shows how NGOs are playing an important role in achieving all the above mentioned objectives.

Brinda Karat, the well known feminist leader, who has been the general secretary of AIDWA for more than a decade writes in her book, Survival and Emancipation, Notes from Indian Women's Struggles (2005) about the feminist movement in India. The work is conveniently grouped into six sections each around a distinct theme, such as strategies adopted by AIDWA over time; globalization and survival issues; political participation; women's interface with communalism, and violence against women. The book ends on a personal note recounting the rich experiences of the author in college. The women's movement has been grappling with certain problematic issues, which have time and again created confusion over the movement's agenda and status. Today the Dalits, tribals and marginalized women have innumerable agencies espousing their cause but real empowerment remains an enigma. Brinda Karat discusses various issues related to women from the Leftist point of view, the Left-led struggle sees the process of ideological struggle as well as concrete practices against all forms of gender-oppression as part of a wider class approach to the different aspects of oppression in Indian society. AIDWA believes that 'women's issues' are not the forte of women alone. Instead women have to struggle with men to fight various forms of injustice. The book discuses reservation for women in politics, gender budgeting by the government and the significance of political influence in women's struggles. Karat does not attempt to enter into complicated epistemological issues instead she encapsulates the reality of the everyday faced by the ordinary woman.

Micro-Credit, Poverty and Empowerment-Linking the triad, (2005) is edited by Neera Burra, Joy Deshmukh–Ranadive and Ranjani K Murthy. The book is a collection of six case studies of governmental and quasi-governmental organizations initiated by UNDP and ICICI Bank to assess the impact of micro-finance activities on women's empowerment and poverty reduction in India. Two persistent problems that affect a significant portion of Indian women are poverty and violation of their human rights. In recent years, micro-credit has come to be viewed as a vital tool to ameliorate both conditions. This book is a pioneering effort, in the Indian context, to test the validity of the assumption that there is a linear link between micro-credit, poverty reduction and women's empowerment. The case studies provide significant findings regarding the potential of micro-credit and the effort of intervening organizations in reducing poverty and empowering women. While poor women have an inherent potential for transformation, an external stimulus seems necessary to unleash the process. In all the case studies reviewed the process of empowerment was fostered by an intermediary organization from outside. The process occurred not through a top-down but a bottom-up strategy that released the creative potential of poor women and other oppressed groups. However such a process cannot be nurtured by the intermediary organisations alone. There are many factors including the women's efforts, in the macro environment which affect empowerment The empowerment impact of micro-credit is higher when an organization chooses to work with women who are oppressed and need support to be empowered. Even so, other factors are also important. The findings show the potential and limitations of micro-credit in reducing poverty and empowering women. It is true that micro-credit programmes improve women's access to economic resources and generic basic needs. It enables them to have access to independent sources of saving and credit. This makes them more self confident and self reliant. However such positive impact comes with qualifiers. Micro-credit interventions have to be sensitive to poverty and gender discrimination, even so there are limits to how far these can reach the ultra poor on their own Various other factors like gender inequalities in domestic and macro environment, inequalities in access to socio-cultural and political spaces and in control over resources within economic spaces, the type of household headship, caste and religion are important in deciding how far micro-credit can improve conditions. Collective strategies beyond micro-credit to increase the endowments of the poor women, enhance their exchange outcomes vis-à-vis the family, state, markets and community, and expand socio-cultural and political spaces, are required for poverty reduction and women's empowerment. Mental spaces of both women and men need to expand to enable such a process.

"Women's Empowerment through Capacity Building-Enduring efforts in Bangladesh" by Ashish Bose (2004) has a Foreword by Ela Bhatt the founder of SEWA, the world renowned women's Trade Union. She writes, Women's empowerment is not merely an "issue" related to women, it is an issue of development of our society as a whole. Women do have power despite their poverty, food insecurity and ignorance; they need to be organized, to realize their full potential.'

Dr Ashish Bose, in this book has captured Dr Zafrullah Chowdhury's vision of health by self reliance and his leaderhip in developing a large cadre of competent health workers as backbone of rural healthcare. It is a brilliant story of capacity building of the rural women giving healthcare to poor masses in rural areas of Bangladesh, through the organization, Ganosasthya Kendra. Important Elements of the GK strategy include the following : (1) capacity building, not charity (every member has to pay an initial fee for books etc., (2) skill formation is essential and everybody can be trained, (3) what men can do women can also do, (4) no gender discrimination at work, (5) vital role of Paramedics, (6) pervading spirit of idealism, patriotism and solidarity. Research and observation shows that GK's experiment in capacity building and empowerment of women is a great success story.

Women and Rural Development Programmes (2004) by Verma and Nath is an attempt to asses the extent to which the Government's development policies and programmes for women under the Five Year Plans have really been able to improve the status and lot of women in Indian society. The authors analyse the impact of various macro policies and programmes on rural women. Emerging conclusions are the need for reorientation of rural development policy in order to bring rural women into the mainstream of development. The book also emphasizes on the need for an effective women's movement for a real breakthrough in the improvement of their status and living conditions.

The book gives detailed account of all major development programmes specifically meant for rural women in India. These include programmes for education, health and nutrition, employment and alleviation of poverty of rural women. Some important ones are DWCRA, NLM, DPED, Mahila Samakhya and Welfare Extension Projects. The authors conclude that in the last five decades of national planning various development programmes have been projected as Government' Programmes and not as peoples' programmes, which is not correct. For rural transformation programmes should emerge from within and not be imposed from above. Any movement for the upliftment of women needs a dynamic approach both from the side of women by exhibiting the right attitude and participation and from the side of the authorities by strengthening the national machinery.

In his book, Women Rural Labourers, Dr Joshi discusses the problems and prospects of rural women workers in Gujarat, on the basis of his research work. The main objectives of his study were to find out the living conditions, working condition, wages and employment and problems of female agricultural workers in his sample which was selected from 8 districts of Gujarat. His main findings were that rural women have two major problems; they are paid less and have irregular employment. They are mostly unskilled which adversely affects wage rate and employment, otherwise in Gujarat females are generally paid at the same rate as males for same type of job. Most of the female labourers were of lower and backward classes, living below poverty line. They are unorganized and have no union. They do not get facilities like sanitation, education, health, rest etc. They are over worked, have health problems and do not have proper housing facilities. Ninety per cent of the sample is illiterate. 70 per cent earn Rs 30 or less per day. Unemployment is higher among females. Two thirds of them are forced to work due to poverty. One third of them are in debt. In the family they do not get the support of other members, most of them give all their earnings to hubands. Most are dissatisfied with their work and would not like their children to do the same. The state of Gujarat is a developed state, but the development is unbalanced resulting in regional differences in economy problems of female labourers are more serious in under developed districts. Their problems are not only monitory but also social and familial. These should be addressed by the Government urgently.

Problems of Women Workers in Unorganised Sectors, by Saran and Sandhwar (1990) is a study of women working in brick kilns, quarries and mines in Bihar and West Bengal. The present work gives an authentic information of the socio-economic and physical exploitation of these women by the employers and their hopeless condition.

The study revealed many instances of violation of human rights and exploitation. About 15 per cent workers were below 16 years of age which is a violation of Child Labour Act. The whole recruitment procedure aims at securing cheap labour in utter violation of Inter-state Migrant Workmen Act and the Contract Labour Act. The migrant women workers in the brick kilns in both states are generally not allowed to leave the job during the season which lasts for six months. They may be considered as bonded labour for that period. Most women live below poverty line and are forced to work due to extreme poverty. More than 90 per cent belong to Scheduled Castes and Tribes and Backward Classes. Most of these women perform unskilled jobs. The working hours of migrant women vary a lot. Generally they work 14-16 hrs a day, but the local women work for 8 hrs a day. Weekly holiday on the basis of 'no work no pay' can be availed on Hat day, but most poor women do not do so. There is no maternity leave nor is there any medical assistance. Workmen Compensation Act is also not followed strictly in case of accidents at the mines or quarries. Sex discrimination in payment of wages is not observed, but rate of actual wages that the women workers receive and the rate of payment which the owners claim to have paid show a greater degree of discrepancy in Bihar than in West Bengal. The Minimum Wages Act is not observed in any of these unorganized sectors. There is no provision for crèches. Rebuking, cheating, threatening, beating and sexual abuses are common in the brick kiln of Bihar. The greatest humiliation to the women workers is pertaining to sexual offences and abuses. The authors conclude that attempts should be made to educate the women and make them aware of their rights. Attention should be paid to strict implementation of various labour Acts. Welfare measures in the unorganized sector should be entrusted to voluntary organizations.

The Research Centre for Women's Studies at SNDT University has published three volumes entitled; Assistance for Women's development from National Agencies, as users' guide for needy women. The first one is about Employment Programmes, the second about Housing Programmes and the third about Development Programmes. Buxamusa and Gupte have provided very useful and relevant information in these volumes. In the guide on Housing Programmes they give details of schemes like Indira Awas Yojana, Rescue Homes, Government Protective Homes, Grant-in-aid for Hostel Building, and other schemes being implemented in Maharashtra. The book also gives information about loan facilities fron National Housing Bank and Housing Development Finance Corporation.

In her book, 'Women and Society' (2005) Zainab Rahman discusses the status of women through the ages and gives reasons for the subordinate position generally alloted to them. She writes that although women do as much or even more work than men, they are not given equal recognition or remuneration mainly because most of women's work does not fetch cash and secondly in a patriarchal setup women are not given any importance and all their hard work at home and elsewhere is taken for granted, not being recognised as 'work' at all. She discusses the role of women in different areas of life and highlights their contribution in each. She writes about the role of rural women as follows; 'The life of the rural poor is very tough and women bear the brunt of this struggle for survival. They not only work at home but in the fields, the forests, with the household animals and also carry on cottage industries. They play a significant role in agriculture, in forestry, in environmental conservation and in the Panchayats'. An entire chapter has been devoted to women of Uttaranchal in which the hard work of rural women of the hills is highlighted.

Micro Finance for Women (2005) by S N Dhar deals with the concept of Micro-finance and its development implications as well as its impact on women's empowerment. The book deals with concepts of micro-finance, systems of micro-finance delivery, i.e., the linkages of self help groups with banks and impact of micro-finance schemes on women using socio-economic indicators. It gives an account of the role played by a regional Rural bank in North Bengal in formation and linking of SHGs. It also deals with the perceptions of women micro-entrepreneurs towards micro-financing and also with their problems. The author writes that inspite of Governmental measures the participation of women in the economy has not increased adequately. More than 90% women work in the informal sector. There are two ways in which women can get opportunity to work : either through wage employment or through self-employment. It is being felt that self employment, supported by credit has more potential for improving the asset base of the poor women in the long run than wage-employment. Generation of self-employment among very poor rural women, or in other words promotion and development of micro-entrepreneurship among rural women is a strategy for long term sustainable socio-economic improvement. Since the mid-80s women as micro and small entrepreneurs have received increased attention and assistance by governments, NGOs and international donors. The term micro-finance originated in 1944 when the cooperative movement started in Germany, but it actually gained sensitization and generated awareness in the mid 90s after the World Summit for Social Development was held in Copenhagen in 1995. This summit underscored the significance of access to credit to low income women and to vulnerable groups. Micro finance aims at increasing women's income levels and control over income leading to greater level of econmic independence and also women's participation in household decisions and other benefits. These can be better achieved if women work in groups and inculcate the practice of self help. A SHG borrows from a bank and uses it according to its own planning for income generation. The savings generated by the members are re-lent among them selves creating a second loan portfolio whose interest becomes an additional source of income to the borrowers. Micro-finance does alleviate poverty but empoerment does not only include an increase in women's levels of income, but control over income and assets and participation in community and household decisions. The author concludes that the benefits of the micro finance programme conducted by UBKGB for women, have to some extent percolated in the rural areas, but there are some impediments to entrepreneurial development like, ignorance, illiteracy, unhygienic conditions etc. that should be addressed.

In her book, Women, Gender, Equality and the State, (2000) Sadhna Arya writes about the various measures taken by the Indian Government to improve the lot of women. She writes, ' the Govt. of India gave importance to women over national economic projects under pressure, after 1975 in its planning. The measures included various schemes for women, setting up of Women's Development Corporations, strengthening existing agencies and help in income generation activities. The shift in policy from welfare to development led to delienation of the role of WDC, in providing education and income facilities and the role of CSWB in providing supporting services like creches, homes etc. The various approaches to women's issues that have been adopted are as follows :

1. **Poverty alleviation and income generation** : Programmes like IRDP, DWCRA and TRYSEM were included in this approach. DWCRA was different from others as it was a total women's programme and emphasised non-economic activities. Shram Shakti, the report given by NCSW in 1988 evaluated these programmes.

2. Women in Development approach premised that women had been neglected in the development process and that there is need to make effective use of women as human resource. In this approach stress is to be laid on education, employment, equality and empowerment of women. In the decade 1975–85 education and employment received much attention.

3. **Participation and Empowerment approach :** Income generation programmes revealed that the status of women, their fertility, nutrition and health and other development indicators are linked with literacy and education opportunities. Improvement in one or two sectors is not enough. Thus a new approach extended the meaning of development

> from bringing in benefits to also changing social attitudes which prevent backward women from participating in development activities to achieve empowerment. It was planned that women should be empowered through groups, raising awareness and providing economic and social support services

In the last twenty years the Government policies have had mixed success. The policies, made to improve conditions, have not been effective in addressing women's issues like equality. The author concludes that State accountability has to be stressed. There has to be a change in perspective, in order to give importance to equality and gender justice. Women perform both productive and reproductive roles so they need more support services.

Neeta Tapan, in her book, 'Need for Women's Empowerment' gives an account of all the schemes being run by the Government and NGOs to improve women's lot but she notes that women are still not empowered and gender equality and justice are yet to be achieved. She gives details of the various forms of gender discrimination that exist in our society and that hinder the progress of women. She also rightly points out that women themselves are to some extent responsible for this discrimination so they have to make an effort to change their attitude and liberate themselves from the socio-cultural quagmire. She writes, 'It is estimated that in the rural areas a girl works for 10 hours a day, providing the family an annual labour of about Rs 2000 and by the time she grows up she contributes about Rs 40,000 to family income by her labour. Girls start assisting in collecting firewood, fuel and fodder, fetching water and looking after younger siblings, at an early age. Even in the traditional economic model rural women contribute invisibly to the economic development of the nation.' The author concludes that women should be provided better health care, education facilities and many other basic facilities so that they can make progress and contribute to national development.

Anjali Bahuguna in her book, 'Science and Technology in relation to Rural Women' emphasises the need to train women in new technology so that they may get better employment and earn more. She writes about UNIFEM which has two mandates :

1. To act as a catalyst for mainstreaming women into development and
2. To give direct support to innovative and experimental projects

The fund is aiding many innovative projects for rural women. The author writes that Indian planning has given priority to teaching science and technology to rural women in suitable ways to improve efficiency and income. "India's prime need is the use of science and technology as a powerful tool for the benefit of the masses in the rural areas rather than enriching a few upper class farmers." Accoring to the Approach to 8th Five Year Plan, ' Improvement in the wellbeing of the mass of the people will require substantial inputs from science and tecnology. Importance was also given to research for finding out solutions to locally specific problems on a project basis, adaptation of relevant technologies to suit local conditions, demonstration of such adapted technologies through centres and imparting skills required to utilise these technologies in day to day life, through training centres. She concludes that rural women need to be given training as well as education in order to participate in development activities and in politics and thus empower themselves.

Rural Muslim Women–Role and Status, is a study by Sekh Rahim Mondal, in North Bengal. He writes that the women in his sample are not economically independent. They are responsible for the indoor activities and the home is their domain. They have a say in domestic decisions but not in decisions of consumption and production. Women do all the housework and take care of children, besides participating in gardening, animal and fowl rearing, water fetching and firewood gathering. Illiteracy and low education is quite rampant although some positive changes are taking place due to modernization and younger generation is getting education. He writes that although Muslim women do not have a high social status on the basis of their economic, educational or organizational attributes, they have an important social position due to their role in family management, retention of culture and heritage. Men dominate in public and community affairs and have the decision making power as heads of households, while women enjoy greater freedom and say in family and domestic life. This public and domestic dichotomy based on gender difference is the reflection of patriarchy in Muslim society. The concept of patriarchy in Muslim society conveys respect and cohesion rather than conflict between sexes. Muslim women play an invisible role in their society but have concealed power and position in functioning of the society. They are respected for their domestic role but are also exploited in many ways.

Rural Landless Women Labourers (2005) is a study by A. Balakrishnan in a District of Tamil Nadu. He gives a detailed account of the socio-economic status of his respondents and focusses on their problems. He writes that according to 1991 census the percentage of rural work force engaged in agriculture and allied activities contributed about 40% of net domestic production. These agricultural labourers lead a life of absolute poverty and are the most backward and exploited class of the rural economy. They are the weakest link in the chain of rural economy and attention needs to be paid to their problems immediately for real progress to take place in rural sector. Most of the women in the sample were married women and worked as agricultural labourers. Their literacy rate was low and awareness level still lower. Nearly half lived below poverty line. They face the problem of seasonal unemployment and are mostly daily wage earners which shows the temporary nature of their jobs. They are paid less than men and sometimes are not paid promptly. About half of them were not paid for overtime work. Very few had basic facilities at work place. Only 1.6% respondents were aware of Minimum Wages Act. At home their condition is better as most of them get the support of their husbands in various ways. They have a role in decision making. The children of 85% women were attending school. The author concludes that these women should get better facilities of health and education and should be given training for taking up skilled labour. Their awareness of development programmes should also increase.

The SEWA Movement and Rural Development, by Daniel W Crowell, gives a detailed accout of the origin, development and various activities of the famous women's Union, SEWA. The book deals specifically with the SEWA initiative in Banaskantha and Kutch. The SEWA movement started in Ahmadabad in Gujarat. A Gandhian, Ela Bhatt, who was incharge of the women's wing of TLA, started a union of women working in the unorganised sector, named Self Employed Women's Association, as a branch of TLA in early 70s. It organised the illiterate poor women, working as cart pullers, head loaders, rag pickers, vegetable vendors etc. to work jointly for their rights and to safeguard their interests. SEWA aims at increasing employment opportunities and income of its members and providing them better access to health, nutrition and other basic facilities. It also aims at increasing their strength, self-reliance, leadership qualities and assets, so that they are truly empowered. SEWA lays stress on capital formation and capacity building for the poor women so that they may have better employment opportunities and options. This gives bargaining power to the women. The SEWA family is made up of 220,000 members and 16 organisations. The organizers and administraters are dedicated workers and are also members of SEWA. They run their own Sahkari Bank and have also started insurance scheme recently. SEWA also forms linkages between its members and the Government's rural development programmes. It is a success story of the effc ts of poor uneducated women to fight for their rights and improve their lot collectively.

Women, Poverty and Resources (1990) is a book written by Wigmaraja Ponna. It discusses the plight of poor women who have skills and also the acumen to start a business but lack capital. The author writes that there should be some special credit facilities for such women as the conventional system of credit is not easily approachable for them. There has to be some new and easy system for them to get loans. In Gujarat and in the South there are loan facilities for the poor but in Uttarakhand, where women are quite aware and willing to do business, they lack capital. A holistic and flexible approach to intervention helps in addressing this regional diversity, while maintaining the focus on women in the informal sector.

Encyclopaedia of Women's Studies, Vol. 2 is entitled Women and Work and has accounts of rural women at work One such study is by Karen Kapadia. It is a study of Pallar women in Tamil Nadu conducted in 1988. Her main findings were : women work harder than men, have stable jobs and are more independent of men than women of higher castes but they are exploited by their own men and the landlords, economically. They play dual role, still their work is not recognised due to social conditioning and mode of conceptualising women's work. The work of these low class, landless labourer women in agriculture is largely unrecognised in economic surveys. These women contribute all their earnings to the household whereas the men don't. Men are frustrated because due to mechanisation they do not find proper jobs and do not want to do feminine jobs, hence they resort to drinking and violence and the burden of family survival falls on the shoulders of women. Wages are low and lower for women, so while the Pallar labourers get impoverished, the capitalist agricultural producer becomes richer at their expense.

In her book, Duaghters of The Earth, Smita Tiwari Jassal, discusses the issue of women and land rights in Uttar Pradesh. She has conducted studies in different villages among the poorest women to find out how hard they work for survival, not only their own, but that of their families. Although these poor households were to get land under land redistribution scheme they do not possess any land. Women contribute equally, if not more, than men in agriculture and food production but they are missing as a category from most studies on agrarian societies in India. Women's invisibility as significant contributors in agrarian production is a characteristic feature of Indian socio-historical studies. She says that denial of property rights to women is a significant instrument of patriarchy so much so that the legal title to land, access to it as a productive resource and the ability to exercise control over it and enjoy the fruits of one's labour on it, is generally denied to Indian rural women. This, inspite of the various legislations and Government schemes, is a glaring example of gender injustice.

Conditioning and Empowerment of Women–A Multidimensional Approach (2003) has been edited by Mukherjee and Bhattacharya. This book analyses the status of women in India and the alternative modes of their empowerment. The issue of empowerment is viewed from different dimensions by well known feminist writers. It deals equally with the theoretical issues relating to empowerment as well as issues involved in practice. There are articles on women's role in Panchayat, Environment management, joint forest management etc. Various authors have given their conception of the word Empowerment. Purkayastha writes that women have multiple and diverse interests through out the world and women's rights as human rights cannot be based on a state of individual rights alone. Women's rights have to be conceptualised as a set of multi layered identities and gender rights attending to the needs of the individual and her position as a member of a group. Chaudhuri writes that although reservation for women in local bodies is meant to empower women, her survey in a Bengal village shows women are not full empowered, specially at home they do not have sufficient freedom of action and decision. Most women were not interested in contesting elections and generally men acted in the name of their wives who were elected. She writes male cooperation is essential to really empower women. At the moment, she writes, rural women are becoming more conscious of their responsibilities and rights but they have a long way to go to act as successful political leaders.

'Women and Politics is edited by Kiran Saksena. In the Introduction she gives a historical background of women's movement and stresses the need for empowering women. She writes, ' there is unanimity amongst all the feminists that women are handicapped because they are bereft of power, therefore they should be empowered.' The core of politics is the exercise of power; politics belongs to the public sphere where intrusion of women is forbidden. This is not just or democratic hence feminists demand women's participation in politics. Indian feminist movement was successful in getting the 73rd amendment passed, obtaining reservation for women in local bodies. But for empowerment to be real, it has to be treated as a multi-faceted concept allowing decision making power to women in all areas. Reservation in some political institutions is not sufficient. Different authors have described the role of women in politics based on their studies. A study in Meerut, UP, concludes that the very low socio-economic position of women does not enable the Pradhanis of the sample villages to participate in the functioning of the Panchayats. Their lack of education and low participation in public life has limited their role to the household. They are not aware of developmental programmes and also lack various skills. What is worse is that the patriarchal structure of society makes it impossible for them to learn Women continue to play a minimal role in Panchayats so that the author concludes that reservation has not led to women participating in decision making in local bodies. Another author points out that the SHG experience has empowered women economically and organised them in groups thus making them more self confident so they can be better elected representatives. They are likely to hold their elected Panchayat more responsible for its decisions.

Gender and Caste (2003) edited by Anupama Rao makes explicit the ways in which Dalit women's movements have contributed to unique feminist positions in India, inadequately acknowledged in the mainstream. Dalit women's subjugation is characterised by their experience of two distinct patriarchal structures/situations : a brahmanical form of patriarchy that deeply stigmatized dalit women because of their caste status, as well as the more intimate forms of control by Dalit men over the sexual and economic labour of their women. Indian feminism has, for long, rendered this undercurrent invisible. Dalit women demand that Indian feminism should be made more representative and inclusive by including dalit women's 'difference' from the ideal subjects of feminist politics. In the 1990s there were several independent and autonomous assertions of dalit women's identity; a case in point is the formation of the National Federation of Dalit Women and the All India Dalit Women's Forum. This has led to a major debate, whether Dalit women talk differently. Of course there are differences in the socio-cultural and economic lives of high caste and dalit women, hence their need to talk differently. The book ends with the NGO Declaration on Gender and Racism by NFDW, presented at Durban in 2001 at the World Conference against Racism, which condemns caste and gender based discrimination agaist dalit women.

Globalization (2004) edited by Malini Bhattacharya presents the effects of globalization on women. In a country like India, which abounds in diversity, it is not easy to enforce the kind of uniformity that globalization envisages. It affects prevailing patriarchal system and the lineaments of gender relationships at various levels. It has special implicatins for women because they are responsible for upholding and preserving traditional identities. The changes brought about by globalization have to some extent benefited educated, urban women but they have been detrimental to the condition of rural women. With regard to agriculture, globalization has tended to favour cash crops over food crops, to the detriment of women and family nutrition. Distribution of resources essential for cash crops and the process of mechanisation have gone against the interests of rural women in their efforts to produce adequate food supplies. In women-centred agriculture sustainability is ensured and genetic base of food production is carefully maintained. Globalization has hit hard at the root of this age old ethics of conservation, as it has marginalized women in agriculture. In the last decade, NSS data show that there was a drop in the share of the self employed, for rural men and women and a rise in the share of both regular employees and casual labourers. Self employed rural women would mostly be uneducated, coming from agricultural families, hence they can only become casual labourers on losing their work, thus they are subject to downward mobility in economy. Sexual division of labour in our country adds to the woes of rural women. Globalization has not only affected rural women's employment adversely, it has also had a bad effect on the unpaid household work of women by making it more streneous. The book discusses how globalization has affected presentation of women in the media, women rural artists and so on.

Aspects of Women and Development is edited by Khan, Saigol and Zia. It presents the Pakistani women's experience with modern development. There is also a study of rural women of Panjab in this connection. The editors write that the dominant, economic models of development as promoted by the IMF Structural Adjustment Programmes and the World Bank have had contradictory, if not outright negative, effects on women. Class and gender differences seem to be increasing with the application of the dominant paradigms of development, leading to inequalities which are a negation of fundamental human rights. Various papers in this book discuss the status of Pakistani women and hold the society, the norms and patriarchal values responsible for the negation of women's human rights and other problems. The main conclusion of the study on effect of development on rural women was that it has affected women negatively. Mechanization has led to unemployment of women. New trend of cash drops has marginalised women in agriculture, thus lowering their status and depriving them of the feeling of being a part of the land. Nuclear family system has also caused loneliness and emotional deprivation.

K P Neeraja, in her book, Rural Women, discusses the health care available to women and children in villages and bases her conclusions on the study she conducted in a district of Andhra Pradesh. She writes that inspite of various governmental efforts in rural areas, health of women and children is a major cause of concern. This is because the women are not aware of facilities available and also because facilities are not easily available to them. Important programmes being run for rural women and children are many; some of them are Rural Health Scheme, Family welfare Programme, Pulse Polio Programme, Reproductive and Child health Programme. Many Laws and Policies are also there to improve the health of these target groups. The main findings were that utilisation of ante natal, natal and post natal services was in declining order. Factors like education, occupation, caste, frequency of visits by Health Personnel influenced the utilisation rate. Awareness of Family planning measures and immunisation of children was high and majority of women got their children immunised.

Informal Economy Centrestage is a book about workers in the informal sector. It is edited by Jhabvala, Sudarshan and Unni. It defines informal sector and informal employment as follows : The System of National Accounts (1993) characterises the informal sector as consisting of units engaged in the production of goods or services with the primary objective of generating employment and income to the persons concerned. It is part of the household sector, owned by households. Informal employment is employment created outside the recognised institutional framework. Informal sector workers may be self employed or wage earners. Women form the bulk of informally employed workers. 94% of the women workers are engaged in the unorganised sector of the economy. These women are unprotected by labour laws. The book gives an account of the pioneering work of the famous SEWA.

Education and Socio-Economic Perspectives of Women Development and Empowerment, is written by Aruna Goel. She writes about the discrimination women face in employment and in the economy, specially in this age of globalisation, privatisation and liberalisation. She suggests that Government should impart excellent vocational and educational training to women so that they can compete with men. She also writes about the various rural development schemes which are meant to empower women but have not been able to do so to the full extent due to poor implementation.

In Garhwal Himalaya, a book edited by Kandari and Gosain, Himanshu Borai writes about the hill women. She writes that the majority of the population of Garhwal is engaged in agriculture and allied activities and women's contribution is more than that of men in this regard. They are deeply involved in agriculture at all stages. They are also involved in livestock rearing and fuel and fodder collection. They also engage in cottage industries like woolen products. They work hard at home, in the fields and in community activities. They form the backbone of Garhwal economy.

Besides the boks mentioned above the researcher has referred to various other books on empowerment of women. Some of them are, Women's Empowerment-Issues Challenges and Strategies [2005] by Kumar H and Varghese J, Empowerment of Women [2002] by Grover and Grover, Empowering Rural Women–Issues, Opportunities and Approaches [2005] edited by Samanta R K and

Empowerment-Sustainable Human Development Strategy for Poverty Alleviation [2004] by Puthenkalam J J. All these books deal with various aspects of women's empowerment and discus ways and means to achieve it.

## Conclusion

We have seen how women are given a lower position than men inspite of their important contributions to society and inspite of legal equality being granted to them by many States. We have also seen how modern development has not helped women as it was intended to, instead it has had a negative effect on masses of lower class women. Rural women specially have been the worst victims. The review of literature also shows that rural women generally face many problems, discriminations and injustices. Due to their low literacy level and lack of awareness they are not able to benefit through various development schemes. Review of literature has also shown how various methods are being employed by Government and NGOs to help rural women get empowered. Many authors have given detailed descriptions of efforts by Government and NGOs to empower women while others have pointed out the difficulties and hindrances in empowering women. Some books have described the experiences of specific movements and projects in improving the lot of women. Since this study is of rural women, most books reviewed are about rural women in particular. These women need to be empowered urgently and it is heartening to note that both the Government and the NGOs are committed to this onerous task and rural women too are making conscious efforts to empower themselves.

## References

1. Malini Bhattacharya 2004 Globalization Tulika Books.
2. Shiva Vandana 1987 Staying Alive Kali for Women.

3. Ministry of HRD Working Group on Empowerment of Women–Tenth Plan.
4. Joel SGR Bose 2003 NGOs and Rural Development Concept Publishing.
5. Narsimhan Empowering women Sage Publications.
6. Ministry of H R D Platform for Action. India Country Report.
7. Laxmi Devi A 1987 Rural Women Northern Book Centre.
8. Sinha AK 2004 Panchayati Raj and Empowerment of Women. Northern Book Centre.
9. Bhose Joel SGR 2003 NGOs and Rural Development Concept Publishing.
10. Karat Brinda 2005 Survival and Emancipation Three Essays.
11. Burra, Ranadive, Murthy (Ed) Micro credit, Poverty and Empowerment 2005, Sage Publication.
12. Bose Ashish 2004 Empowerment through Capacity Building Samskriti.
13. Verma & Nath 2004 Women and Rural Development Programmes, B R Publishing Corporation.
14. Joshi M V 1999 Women Rural Labourers.
15. Saran & Sandhwar 1990 Problems of Women Workers in Unorganised Sector, Northern Book Centre New Delhi.
16. Baxamusa & Gupte 1992 Assistance for Women's Development–Housing Programmes Popular Prakashan Bombay.
17. Rahman Zainab 2005 Women and Society Kalpaz Publication.
18. Dhar S N 2005 Micro Finance for Women Northern Book Centre.
19. Arya Sadhana 2000 Women, Gender, Equality and the State, Deep and Deep Publications.

20. Tapan Neeta 1998 Need for Women's Empowerment Rawat Publication.

21. Bahuguna Anjali (Ed) Science and Technology in relation to Rural Women, 1990 Har Anand Publication.

22. Mondal Sekh Rahim 2005 Rural Muslim Women Norther Book Centre.

23. Balakrishnan A 2005 Rural Landless Women Labourers Kalpaz Publication.

24. Crowell Daniel W 2001 The SEWA Movement and Rural Development Sage Pub.

25. Wigmaraja Ponna 1990 Women Poverty and Resources Sage Publications.

26. Kapadia Karen 1988 Encyclopaedia of Women's Studies Vol 2 Women and Work.

27. Jassal Smita Tivari 2001 Daughters of the Earth Manohar.

28. Mukherjee & Bhattacharya Conditioning and Empowerment of Women, 2003, Gyan Publishing House.

29. Saksena Kiran (Ed) Women and Politics Gyan Publishing House.

30. Rao A (Ed) 2003 Gender and Caste Kali for Women.

31. Bhattacharya M 2004 Globalization Tulika Books.

32. Khan, Saigol, Zia (Eds) 1995 Aspects of Women and Development ASR Publication.

33. Neerja KP 2000 Rural Women Discovery Publishing House.

34. Jhabvala, Sudarshan, Unni Informal Economy Centrestage Sage Publications, [Eds] 2001.

35. Goel Aruna Education and SocioEconmic Perspectives of Women's, 2003, Development and Empowerment Deep and Deep.

36. Kandari & Gosain (Eds) Garhwal Himalaya TransMedia

Shrinagar.

37. Samanta RK [Ed.] 2005 Empowering Rural Women-Issues, Opportunities and Approaches The Women Press.

38. Dutta R K 2000 Women Empowerment Reference Press.

39. Grover and Grover 2002 Empowerment of Women Geeta Somani Agrotech Publishing Academy Udaipur.

40. Kumar Hajira & Varghese J Women's Empowerment–Issues Challenges and Strategies [2005] Regency Publication.

41. Puthenkalam J J 2004 Empowerment–Sustainable Human Development Strategy for Poverty Alleviation Rawat Publications Jaipur & Delhi.

# 2

# Methodology

This chapter presents a theoretical frame to explain the reasons for the subordinate position allotted to women in all cultures and societies and the efforts that have been made by feminists to achieve the rightful place of womanhood or half of humanity, in society. In recent past efforts are being made by world bodies and governments to establish gender justice and equality by adopting various measures. The idea is that women are powerless so they should be empowered. In explaining all this the present research has made use of many concepts which will also be clarified in this chapter. After dealing with the theory, we will describe the research methodology, or the detailed outline of the research work. This will include description of the research design, the objectives and hypothesis, the universe and sample, the techniques and tools used for data collection, classification and analysis.

**Theoretical Frame :** Since time immemorial men and women have lived together, worked together, produced children and taken care of them. Man-woman relationship is the basic and primary human relationship. At the dawn of humanity people lived in groups in a form of community livelihood. There was no concept of private property. Relations between sexes were based on reciprocity. The process of reproduction of the species gave women the special power of dominance over the community. It gave rise to matriarchy so long as means of production, consumption and distribution were collective.[1] Once man started settled life and collected private property, he became aware of his physical strength. He became aquisitive and possessive. Gradually division of labour based on sex was institutionalised and women were confined to homes and were subordinated. Since then history shows, women have been given a lower status than men in all societies. They work as much as, or even more than, men but still their work is not given equal importance. They are discriminated against, exploited and oppressed in myriad ways in the name of tradition, religion and social norms. Feminism is a movement to assert the interests of women as a sex. It is a humanistic concern which wants to liberate women. This movement started in the 18th century in Europe. Later it spread to the whole world and is a vibrant, dynamic movement in the contemporary world. Feminists aver that women had a better position earlier in history which has now deteriorated due to various reasons and has to be re-established. Noted feminist authors, Maithreyi Krishna Raj and Neera Desai write that all feminists are concerned about women's subordination and want to find out its causes. Within the women's movement there have been three major ideological positions described as Liberal, Radical and Socialist feminism. These differ in their analysis of the causes of the subordinate position of women and consequently in their action programmes. Liberal feminism advocates equality and individual freedom. It accepts the sex role differences but contends both sex roles are equal hence women should have equal rights. It does not consider the connection between sexual oppression, sexual division of labour and economic class structure, hence it does not explain women's subordination. Radical feminism on the other hand gives importance to the connection mentioned above and holds patriarchy responsible for women's subordination. Hence they demand the destruction of patriarchy. They believe that roots of subordination lie in the biological family, the hierarchical sexual division of society and sex roles. These facts need to be recognised in order to achieve gender equality. Socialist feminism advocates overthrow of patriarchy along with overthrow of capitalism in order to achieve gender equality because even socialism failed to provide complete equality of sexes. It says women's inferior status is rooted in private property and class divided society. Sexist ideology and structures like the family, maintain women's inferior status. Power is derived from sex and class and manifested in patriarchy and class relations. The major task is to discover the inter dependence of class and patriarchy.[2] Patriarchy, according to Banerjee, is a historically developed cultural ideological force, giving gender relations their specific character in each situation. It helps to construct gender in favour of men.

Women's Studies is an independent disciplne which aims at promoting the interests of women. The driving force behind it is Feminism. To explain the exploitation and oppression of women, Women's Studies offers three main approaches of study; the Marxian, the non-Marxian and the Psycho-analytical approach. According to the Marxian theory, Capitalism produces a certain type of psychoanalytic dynamic which forces women to subjugation. Control over female sexuality as well as household labour lead to women's subjugation. Division of labour by sex is hierarchical and rigid. It favours men, leading to patriarchy, i.e., men's control over women's fertility and labour power. The non-Marxian theory shifts the focus from production relations to the area of reproductive relations, which encompass control over both sexuality and fertility of women. Its main contribution is the use of 'gender' in place of 'sex' These theorists have shown that gender is psycho-socially constructed, while sex is purely biological. Gender roles place more restrictions on women than actually placed by sex; i.e., women may be able to do so many things physically but are not allowed to do so by society, thus restricting their role and status. In order to understand the 'situation of women' Women's Studies uses concepts like power and esteem. Power means strength or control. The state, religion, law and family exercise it and women face it more than men. Feminists feel that since all these agents have been unjust to women, they should be overcome or eliminated. If the subordination of women is due to powerlessness then the focus of feminist struggle is to retrieve this power. According to Socialist feminists powerlessness of women is rooted in four basic structures : those of production, reproduction, sexuality and socialisation of children. Unequal sex roles operate both in family and economy. Unpaid nature of domestic work is another basis of women's oppression.[3]

Now that we are clear about the reasons for women's subordination, we come to the steps that are being taken to improve the lot of women, because in the recent decades it has become clear that although most countries grant legal equality to women they are discriminated against and exploited in many ways. Since its inception, the UN has tried to improve the lot of women. It declared 1975 as International women's year and later the decade 75-85 as women's decade and started various development programmes for women. In India too, the CSWI report, Towards Equality was published in 1974 which showed the unsatisfactory condition of Indian womanhood. This put pressure on the government to give priority to the women's issue in planning and policy making. In the last two decades various steps have been taken in

India to improve women's status, like development schemes DWCRA, Mahila Samriddhi Yojna etc., the setting up of NCW and Rashtriya Mahila Kosh, reservation of 33% seats for women in local bodies' elections, ratification of CEDAW, preparation of National Perspective Plan for women (1988-2000) and National Plan of Action for the Girl Child (1991-2000) and special schemes for women's empowerment in the 9th and 10th Five year plans. In the villages the Self Help Groups and Micro-finance schemes are helping rural women to become self reliant. The year 2001 was declared as Women's Empowerment Year. A Parliamentary Committee on Empowerment of Women was set up to constantly monitor women's issues. Women's organisations and NGOs are also contributing a lot to women's uplift. As a result of all these efforts there has been a positive change in women's status, both in urban and rural areas but a lot remains to be done. There has always been a difference in the development of urban and rural women with the latter having a lower literacy rate and lower status. Hence there is greater need to concentrate on the empowerment of rural women.

Women of rural Garhwal are very hard working and socially and politically active. They are a real asset to their families hence they have a better position than rural women in the plains although their social system is also patriarchal. Due to this system women lag behind men in all spheres but still they have comparatively greater freedom and have played leading role in many social movements. In the absence of men, these women act as household heads and take family decisions. They work in their fields through day till late night, besides doing housework and covering long distances on foot to collect water, fodder and fuel. Women have always been active in community affairs, like guarding community forests, distributing water among villagers during acute shortage, harvesting and cutting from community forests for their needs and organising the worship of community deity. Women of Uttaranchal are known for their role in social and political movements as well as in the world famous Chipko Andolan, which was a successful movement to save the forests and thus conserve the environment. Like all other rural women these women too face many problems which need to be solved. Various schemes for their development and empowerment are being implemented at present.

**Clarification of Concepts** : The major concepts used in this research are as follows :

**Rural Women :** Women who live in villages and whose main occupation is agriculture and allied activities like dairy farming vegetable growing and cottage industries are rural women. Rural women work very hard but have a lower status due to prevalence of patriarchal norms. Most rural women are poor, uneducated and unaware of their rights. They are controlled by their men folk and cannot take their own decisions. But in modern times changes are taking place in the awareness and capabilities of rural women and they are gradually getting empowered. The largest number of working women in India is engaged in farming operations, either as cultivators or labourers in villages.

**Gender Relations :** These encompass the interactions between men and women in various domains and power relations between the two sexes, knowledge of which is necessary to understand the situation of women. Gender relations show the relative social positions of men and women. They are constructed and maintained through a complex array of factors that are formed according to social, cultural and historical circumstances.[4] All norms regarding matters of production, consumption and distribution as well as division of labour are in favour of men. Thus inequality prevails in the gender relationship by assigning a subordinate position to women and not acknowledging their contribution. Gender relations ascribe different attributes, attitudes, desires, personality traits and behavioural patterns to men and women.

**Empowerment :** This is an inclusive term which means not only economic independence but also increase in self confidence and decision making ability. A woman is truly empowered if she can enhance her self confidence and status within her family as independent producer of wealth and provider of finance to her household. Empowerment is a process wherby women gain the ability to make independent choices over their activities and control over resources, become self reliant and overcome subordination.[5]

Thus there are many indicators to measure empowerment of women. The following four variables were selected for the present research.

**Political Participation :** Lester Milbrath has divided society into four categories on the basis of the degree of political participation, namely, those who are apathetic, those who are involved in spectator activities like voting, those involved in transitional activities like attending political meetings and those who enter political arena and stand for or hold party offices. In the present study all four categories of women were identified by data collection.

**Economic Independence :** It means not only earning money but also being able to spend it independently. Control over financial and productive resources, by working women or housewives can be considered economic independence.

**Decision making Ability :** Here again, any woman, whether working or non-working, who can make independent choices and has a say in the decisions made in family and community is said to possess the ability of decision making. It has been noted that women who earn by working outside home have greater decision making ability.

**Access to Basic Facilities :** This includes availability and access to health and hygiene facilities like pure drinking water, sanitation, primary health centre; access to nutritious food, availability of clean and well ventilated homes and satisfaction of minimum needs.

## Methodology

The present study is a micro study of rural women living in ten villages falling under two development blocks in Dehradun district of Uttarakhand. It aims to evaluate the level of empowerment of these women. :

**Objectives of the study** : The main objctives are as follows :

To find out the Socio-economic Status of the women in the ten villages selected for the study

To study the four variables chosen as indices for empowerment of women, namely, (1) the extent of political participation by the women, (2) the extent of economic independence of the women, (3) extent of participation of women in decision making processes and (4) the extent to which women have access to basic facilities in these villages

To find out reasons for either satisfactory or unsatisfactory conditions for women

**Hypotheses** : There are two hypotheses, namely, (1) Rural women in Garhwal participate in politics and decision making processes to a satis factory extent;

(2) Access to basic facilities and econmic independence may not be available to a satisfactory extent due to various ground realities as well as traditional social set up.

**Research Design** : The design for the present research has been formulated on the basis of the aims and objectives of the study. This is mainly a descriptive study which tries to explain the conditions of the sample. A descriptive study is designed to obtain information concerning the current status of phenomenon. The aim is to describe'what exists' with respect to variables or conditions in a situation.[6] It is an exploratory study to the extent that it tries to find out to what extent the women in the sample are empowered. The aproach used is basically structural functional. Data were collected through interview with a view to describe and analyse the various structures and their functions which were related to the four variables under study. On the basis of these data conclusions were drawn.

**Universe** : The universe for the study is Dehradun district of the new State Uttarakhand. It is one of the 13 districts of the State and the capital city Dehradun is also the district head quarters. This district is made up of six developmental blocks, namely, Raipur, Doiwala, Sahaspur, Kalsi, Vikasnagar and Chakrata. The researcher has selected ten villages from the two developmental blocks, Raipur and Doiwala for the study. A sample of 200 women was selected by purposive stratified sampling from these villages.

Dehradun is a beautiful city with pleasant climate and peaceful existance. Since it became the capital of Uttarakhand there has been a lot of devlopment taking place in the form of technology, business, higher education and various industries. New shopping complexes, hotels and educational institutions have come up which point to the progress made in the last few years. Dehradun district has the highest female literacy rate which is 71.22%. Women of Dehradun are quite aware and independent as compared to women of neighbouring states. In Dehradun, the Mayor, the IG Police, the DM and the Post Master General are all women. These facts support the belief that women of Dehradun district are quite active socially and politically and can fend for themselves. The villages that were selected from Raipur block are quite close to the city, hence the liberating influence on women is evident. On the other hand the villages selected from Doiwala are further off hence women there seem to be less liberated. Comparison of data in following chapters will prove this. The details of the ten villages selected for the study are being presentd in the following table.

| *Name of Village* | *Area/sq km* | *House-hold* | *Popula-tion* | *Literates* | *Sch. Caste* | *Sch Tribe* |
|---|---|---|---|---|---|---|
| Ajabpur Kalan | 458.47 | 2288 | 11232 | 7548 | 1186 | 4 |
| Ajabpur Khurd | 187.37 | 383 | 1992 | 1392 | 115 | 0 |
| Mothrowala | 484.82 | 395 | 2132 | 1416 | 05 | 0 |
| Navada | 144.47 | 302 | 1601 | 926 | 103 | 0 |
| Badripur | 178.01 | 313 | 1616 | 953 | 582 | 1 |
| Hansuwala | 68.37 | 50 | 296 | 217 | 39 | 0 |
| Jolly Grant | 839.9 | 1059 | 6316 | 4693 | 357 | 0 |
| Bhanyawala | 273.57 | 428 | 2200 | 1362 | 490 | 9 |
| Majri Grant | 1328.59 | 1180 | 6927 | 4330 | 1110 | 73 |
| Markham Gr. | 2221.3 | 3372 | 19194 | 10513 | 4047 | 1 |

*Source* : Statistical Department, Government of Uttaranchal

The first five villages fall in Raipur block. Ajabpur Kalan and Khurd are very old villages of Dehradun. They are named after Ajba Kunwar Chandel who had helped the Raja of Tehri in the war against Gurkhas. The Raja awarded this land to him. He had two sons, so the land got divided into two villages, namely Ajabpur Kalan and Ajabpur Khurd. The Chandels still are the major landlords in both the areas. There are a sizeable number of Muslims, Nepalis and Scheduled castes living besides Hindus. Ajabpur Khurd has more Hindus and Nepalis. People have pucca houses and condition of women is better as compared to Ajabpur Kalan. The researcher met the descendents of AjbaKunwar who inhabit Ajabpur Kalan and Khurd and are big landlords. They informed that Ajabpur is known for communal harmony and also for allowing scheduled castes inside the temple. There is a famous Mata ka Mandir in Ajabpur where a Harijan priest, Udda Bhakt used to officiate. The Candels were given the title of Rawat and at Jhanda Saheb there was a Rawat Gaddi and at the time of Darbar, the head of Rawats went on an elephant to occupy his seat. These areas have now been declared urban but at the time of research proposal they were villages and the rural atmosphere is still prevalent, mainly because inspite of decrease in agriculture since olden days, agricultural labour continues to be the main occupation of the villagers.

The next village is Mothrowala which is a scenic place surrounded by forests. The rsearcher noticd that there is great communal harmony with Hindus and Muslims sharing the same house as owner and rent payer, in perfect amity. In Dehradun Jhandawala is the place where Shri Guru Ram Rai Darbar Saheb is situated. Every year Jhande ka Mela is held and thousands of people come from different parts of the country to attend it. The Jhanda is mounted on a long bamboo stick which is considered auspicious. This bamboo is cut from the Mothrowala forest which is reached by crossing a river. The other side is known as Lal Dang because the sand there is red. The devotees take the bamboo stick from the Lal Dang forest to Darbar Saheb every three years when the old one is changed for the new one.

Nawada is a little further away from the above three villages. It is also attached to a forest. On a hill in the forest there is an old well and an old Mandir. It is said that the womenfolk of the Chandels used to perform Sati here. Nawada is a developed village. It was named the Swarn Jayanti Village. It has a Panchayat which functions efficiently and implements various development schmes. There is a great number of Nepalis residing in Nawada. The women, specially the Nepali women, are very active politically. At present the Pradhan is a woman who has won a general seat and not a reserved one. Earlier another woman was the Up Pradhan. She is a social worker too. Her name is Anita Thapa. She provided a lot of information. The Block Pramukh also happens to belong to the village and lives there. There are Govt. Primary and Secondary schools, besides private English medium schools. A little further is Kotla which is also a part of Nawada. It is predominantly a Muslim area. This is a backward area and people are poor. Sarva Shiksha Abhiyan is also underway in Nawada.

Badripur is close to Nawada. The Pradhan is a woman but villagers are not happy with her work. There is a Govt. primary school for girls and other private English medium schools. There are some big houses in the village where poor women work as domestic help

The second group of five vilages falls in Doiwala Block. Of all these Markham Grant is the biggest. In fact it includes many small villages which are adjacent to each other. Those which are closer to Doiwala are better developed but remote places like Chandmari and Banjara Basti are not developed. The Pradhan of Markham Grant is Nagina Rani, but the villagers informed that her husband Rameshwar takes all decisions and actions on her behalf. Recently a Congress woman leader came and interviewed the Pradhan and told her that she should increase her knowledge and work on her own. There are both Hindus and Muslims living in these villages and some are quite wealthy. Information was provided by a shopkeper, Mr Naseeb Ahmed.

Hansuwala is a village close to Doiwala and is quite developed. It is inhabited by many Muslims, who are quite prosperous. Their daughters are all educated, some have completed post graduation. There is an inter college and the Doon Ghati College of Professional Education close by. There is a vocational centre named Uttaranchal Shikshan Prashikshan Anusandhan Kendra set up by a local politician some months back. There is also a Sugar Factory near the village.

Bhaniyawala is another village which lies on the main road to Rishikesh. It is a developed and prosperous village with both Hindus and Muslims in good numbers. The Pradhan is the wife of SherSingh but he works as the Pradhan. The researcher met a Ward member, Mr Tauqueer Hussain who provided some information. There is a big Private school named Presidency School, in the village which even has foreign students. There is a college nearby for girls and boys. There is a private vocational centre named Koshish Foundation for women and girls. A lot of information was provided by Raeesa Khatun.

Jolly Grant is again a big village which includes smaller villages. It is quite developed. The airport of Deradun is situated there. The Himalayan Institute of Medical Science which has a big hospital and medical college is also situatd in Jolly Grant. There is a Rajkiya Inter College near the village. There is a primary school in the village Pal Basti. It provides Mid day meals to children. Sarva Shiksha Abhiyan is also going on. There are private English medium schools too.

Teliwala is anothr village with predominantly Muslim population. The Pradhan is a male.

Majri Grant is a village with predominance of Pal caste who are engaged in dairy farming. Ther are big houses belonging to these families. There are also poor people of low castes in the village. Gopal Singh, a dairy farmer and his wife Sunita who is a PhD are running a school named the Himalayan Public School. Three women from this village are ward members, the Pradhan is a male.

After aquainting ourselves with the universe we come to the selection of a sample. for study. It is neither practical nor possible to contact all members residing in a particular area. Therefore generally a researcher bases his inferences on the interviews or tests conducted on a sub-set of the whole. This sub-set is the sample and the aggregate or whole is the population. In the present study also the researcher selected a sample of 200 women from the ten villages to use as respondents in the interviews.

**Sample :** A sample is a representative portion of a whole. Sampling technique is very important in research because it is essential that a representative sample is selected to achieve reliable conclusions. There are many types of sampling techniques, two major types are random sampling and purposive sampling. The researcher adopted purposive sampling because it was more suitable and practical. In purposive sampling the researcher is familiar with the universe hence is able to select a representative sample. In the present case the researcher had made many preliminary visits and a pilot study in order to help in selecting the sample. Secondly stratified sampling was used to make sure that the sample is truly representative. The three variables used for forming the strata were age, education and income. Stratified sampling ensures that the different groups of the population are adequately represented in the sample so that level of accuracy in estimating parameters is increased.[7] Twenty women were selected from each village in such a way that they represented the different age groups, educational levels and economic levels in the proportions in which they are found in these villages.

**Tools and Techniques of Data Collection** : There are various methods of collecting primary data for research work. Some important techniques are observation, questionnaire and interview with a schedule. The researcher used the techniques of interview with an exhaustive schedule as well as observation. Observation is probably the oldest method of enquiry. PV Young defines observation as 'a systematic and deliberate study through the eye of spontaneous occurences at the time they occur.'Whenever the researcher or her team members went for interviews they also observed the respondents' conditions and surroundings in a scientific way.

Interview has been defined by P V Young as a systematic method by which a person enters more or less imaginatively into the inner life of a comparative stranger. It is a face to face contact between the interviewer (researcher or data collector) and the interviewee (respondent or informer) when the former asks questions which are answered by the latter. To make the interview more scientific and systematic a schedule or a set of questions is prepared by the researcher beforehand and it is administered to all respondents in the same way to avoid any bias. The answers are noted down by the researcher himself. Although the process is time consuming it yields excellent results if the interview is performed properly. Secondly it can be used for both educated and uneducated people.

In the present study, an exhaustive schedule was prepared with questions about socio-economic status in the beginning followed by sets of questions related to the different variables to be tested. Finally some questions about general awareness and personal attitudes and aspirations were formulated. This schedule was used by data collectors to collect primary data.

**Process of Data Collection** : The researcher employed five of her research scholars for data collection. These girls were given a week's training to prepare them for conducting the interviews in an objective and effective way. The researcher had earlier met the respondents she had selected. Next she took the data collectors to all the villages to introduce them to the villagers and prospective respondents. These girls were then given the names of the respondents in each village and they distributed the work among themselves and in two and a half months they made 10 visits to the villages to complete data collection. They also took down notes of what all they observed in relation to the objectives of the study. After every visit they reported to the researcher. They found most respondents very cooperative, while a few did not cooperate much. Most of them wanted to know if they would get any governmnt aid when the study was complete. Data collection was done between June and Sptember 2005.

After the formal data collection the researcher once again made separate visits to all the villages with two research scholars who were very dedicated and helpful and were employed for classification and tabulation of data. These visits were made to recheck some facts and also to meet other villagers besides the respondents to find out more about the village and its people. The researcher met Panchayat members, some Pradhans, some social workers, some prestigious families in the villages, school teachers, anganwadi workers, members of self help groups, shop keepers and also some respondents. These visits were very productive as the people already knew about our project and were forthcoming with lots of information in informal chats. All important information was noted down. These visits were spread over a period of few months, i.e., between October 2005 to March 2006.

**Analysis of Data** : After the data was collected it was divided into homogenous and heterogenous groups according to the coding design that had been prepared for this purpose. It was a classification denoting a process of arranging things in groups or classes according to resemblence and affinities and giving expression to the unity of attributes that may exist among diversity of individuals. Then the data was tabulated. Tabulation is the simplest form of representing research findings. Finally the data were interpreted by finding correlations and causal relations among variablesDetailed analysis of various data will be presented in following chapters.

**Significance of the Study** : The present study is very important as women's empowerment is an issue which is centrestage in national planning presently. Such micro-studies provide significant information about the reality of the efforts to empower women. Empowerment is important for all women but since rural women are more oppressed, greater emphasis is on their empowerment, therefore this study will provide valuable data regarding the level of rural women's empowerment and the extent to which various schemes of the Government have been implemented and are successful in empowering women. This information will be useful for planners and implementing authorities as well as for NGOs working with rural women. It will also be a small contribution to the knowledge of rural hill women and their conditions in Women's Studies.

## References

1. Mukherjee and Bhattacharya Conditioning and Empowerment of Women, 2003, Gyan Publishing House.
2. Desai & Krishna Raj Women and Sciety in India Ajanta Books, 1987, International.
3. Rahman Zainab 2005 Women and Society Kalpaz Publications.
4. MondalS R 2005 Rural Muslim Women Northern Book Centre.
5. Dhar SN 2005 Micro-Finance and Women Northern Book Centre.
6. Balakrishnan A 2005 Rural Landless Women Labourers Kalpaz Publications.
7. Nachmias & Nachmias Research Methods in Social Sciences, 1981, St. Martin's Pres New York.

# 3

# Ground Realities of Rural Women and Development Programmes

Women in rural areas have always played a very important role both at home and in the fields. In early rural communities life was tough and no members of the household could be left out of production activities hence women worked side by side with men in fields, in animal husbandry and in family occupations like weaving, handicrafts, pottery etc. The division of labour, although based on sex, was not very rigid and the relationship between sexes was complementary and not one of subordination and domination. Even now in traditional villages women play multifarious roles, but with the sweeping changes brought about in the villages due to modern development and the green revolution, women in Indian villages have lost their earlier importance as producers and are mostly employed as agricultural labourers or petty cultivators. Their cottage industries have also suffered due to industrialization. Still the rural women are the mainstay of rural households and work very hard to sustain themselves and their families. In the hilly regions their work becomes more strenuous due to geographic and socio-cultural reasons.

Women in the hills form the backbone of the village economy and work both at home and in the fields. A great number of men migrate from the villages in search of work and in their absence the women take care of their homes and fields. The hill women are involved at all stages of agriculture. Their household chores are also very arduous and time consuming because they have to cover long, hilly distances to collect fodder and fuel and to get water. A large number of women in forest and tribal areas earn their livelihood by head loading.

In rural India women are still predominantly self-employed/family helpers. The largest number of working women in India are engaged in farming operations either as cultivators or agricultural labourers. The proportion of casual employees, specially in case of women has been increasing in last two decades while self employment is decreasing. Women's contribution to the economy remains valuable but it goes unrecognised. Many feminists and other writers have noted this fact and consider the unpaid nature of most of the work done by women as the main cause of this lack of recognition. In villages women are also engaged in home-based production. They work long hours to make some money and if they are doing piece-rate work then they are exploited by employer as well as middle men. Even the women who work as labourers are not paid same as men for the same work in many villages. The employers exploit women workers economically in many ways and so do their own menfolk. Hence rural women, inspite of working hard and even earning money, are mostly economically dependent on their menfolk. It has also been noted that the rate of unemployment is higher among women than among men, mainly because they are unskilled and today some technical training is required for finding employment. Rural female labourers face many problems. More than 90% of total female workforce operates in the unorganised sector which includes agriculture and agriculture-related work. These workers in unorganised sector are not covered by labour laws and hence they are exploited in many ways, do not have job security, do not have facilities like maternity benefits or social security and have no union.

In the last few decades efforts are being made both at international and national levels to improve the conditions in rural areas and promote and enhance women's participation on an equal basis with men in the proces of rural development so that they too share fully the improved conditions in the villages. This was reiterated in the recommendations of the World Conference on Agrarian Reform and Rural Development, 1979. It was also observed at the Conference that, 'the situation of rural women has now been identified as one of the critical manifestations of the growing imbalances, which constitutes a threat not only to the development of the female population but to the socio-conomic progress of the nations themselves. The National Institute of Rural Development and the F. A. O Workshop on the Integration of Women in Agriculture and Rural Development 1980, observed that 'there is an urgent need to expand knowledge and statistical data on all aspects of the rural poor, particularly with regard to women's role in rural activities and to disseminate this information in order to promote greater awarenes of women's role in society'.[1]

**Rural Development and Women** : The Indian Government gave top priority to rural devlopment soon after independence in the national planning. In the First Five Year Plan a special programme for rural development, namely, Community Development Programme was introduced on 2nd

October 1952. Fifty five projects were started all over India in the nature of pilot experiments. The objective of these projects was multi purpose rural development. A year later these projects were supplemented by a less intensive scheme of development known as National Extension Service which was started all over India on 2nd October 1953. In the early years rural development meant growth of agricultural and allied sectors like animal husbandry, dairying, fisheries, forestry and infrastructural facilities such as drinking water, hospitals, schools, roads and electrification. Over the years rural development has emerged as a strategy designed to improve the economic and social life of a specific group of people, the rural poor. The Community Development programme was designed to promote better living for the whole community with an active participation and, if possible, initiative of the community, but it had no special provisions for the integration of rural women into development, originally. Later it was felt that a special programme for women is needed to make the whole programme more efficient and successful because women have an important role in agricultural decisions and activities. Rural extension work for village women was undertaken by a number of Home Science Colleges. The programme for women and children was meant to make 'home improvements' and the Mahila Mandal Scheme was devised to facilitate this. In the various programmes of CDP women were not given any special focus although they were the weaker section and needed attention.[2] After CDP a more streamlined programme, IRDP was introduced for rural dvelopment and specially for poverty alleviation in 1980. This programme did benefit women to some extent through programmes like DWCRA and TRYSEM. Nearly half the beneficiaries of NREP also were women. A new programme RLEGP, Rural Landless Employment

Guarantee Programme was started in 1983 to focus on landless labourers and it generated additional employment to women in the lean period.

Following the Sixth and Seventh Plans the Department of Rural Development issued directives to the State Governments to give priority to women headed households, enhance the share of women under the anti-poverty programme and to envisage increasing participation of women in wage employment and creation of assets specific to the needs of women's groups. The Government has adopted various policies which aim at creating an enabling environment for properly reflecting, articulating and addressing women's concerns seriously. The important women-related policies include the National Policy on Education, 1986, National Health Policy, 1983 National Population Policy 1993, and National Nutrition Policy 1993. In the following Plans too, the Government gave priority to women's issues and women's empowerment. The various schemes started for women in recent years are many. Some important ones are : Balika Samriddhi Yoja, Kishori Shakti Yojna, Mahila Samakhya, Mahila Shiksha Kendra, Nari Adalat, Swayam Siddha and IWEP [Integrated Women's Empowerment Programme] . Formulation of policies and schemes is not as important as their proper implementation so that the target groups benefit by them. This is where weakneses are noticed, hence more attention has to be paid to implementation of programmes. One of the latest schemes for empowerment of rural women is the formation of SHG [self-help-groups] where women get together to start some small enterprise with micro-credit from banks like NABARD [National Bank of Agriculture and Rural Development] or others. Dhar writes, 'Self-help-groups are voluntary asociations of people, formed to attain certain goals, both economic and social. They are generally formed by the poor coming from rural or semi-urban areas. The basic principle on which a SHG is formed is micro-savings.'[3] At present more than 2000 such SHGs are operating in the country and 90% of these are run by women. Two important legislations enacted in 2005 which will affect rural women are, the Unorganised Sector Workers' Social Security Bill and the National Rural Employment Guarantee Act. The Social Security Bill will cover the entire country and all workers in unorganied sector with monthly income of 5,000/- and below. It covers self employed workers, wage workers, home-based workers and small farmers. The benefits include, minimum social security cover comprising (1) old age pension for workers above 60 years, (2) health insurance for self, spouse and small children, (3) maternity benefits for women and (4) insurance to cover death and disability arising out of accident. According to the NREGA the Government will provide atleast 100 days of guaranteed employment [unskilled, manual work] per year to every rural household in India.

**Effect of Development Programme on Rural Women** : It is not possible to explain all the steps being taken by the Government and NGOs for the empowerment of rural women because the schemes are related to different aspects of rural life and some are not exclusively for women but affect them. Here we are trying to discuss the major, important initiatives of Governmental and non-governmental agencies to affect the lives of rural women positively in various ways. Many authors have given these details in their studies of rural women. AK Singh has given an account of the work done by both agencies for rural women in his book, Empowerment of Women in India [2000]. He writes that out of nearly 6,000 voluntary agencies engaged in social work, about 600 are working in rural areas. Voluntary organisations have many advantages over government agencies because they give a feeling of human touch, are nearer to the community, can ensure mutual aid and speed of implementation, are flexible and can provide the right perspective for social problems, but they need governmental help to run efficiently. The two agencies should work in coordination to achieve best results. Three main forms of government assistance needed are investigational, technical and financial. Women's organisations have been successful in raising consciousness of women's issues and the role of women in development. The role of Voluntary organisations in women's development has also been recognised and the government has started involving them in policy matters as well as implementation of programmes. Voluntary organisations have been given financial assistance by CAPART, [Council for Advancement of Rural Technology] to run various projects aimed at income-generating activities for rural women. They are also helpful in implementing Government programmes like DWCRA. The biggest problem is lack of motivation among beneficiaries. There is also need to provide a complete package of infrastructural facilities. The voluntary organisations also face many problems and shortcomings which need to be addressed.[4]

We will now review the effect of macro-policies related to rural development on rural women. The three important natural resources of land, forest and water are inter-related and any project regarding one affects the other. The land reform policy was a great blow to women because it gave land titles to men. Women, who have traditionally played an important role in land use, have extremely limited access to ownership of land.

The policy of water resource management has also not been in favour of women, since more importance is given to irrigation purposes and water for drinking and household consumption becomes scarce. This causes great hardship to poor rural women because water is central to their lives.

The lives of poor women are closely linked with forests. They depend on forests for fodder, fuel and raw material for economic activities. Due to industrial demands forest cover in the country decreased and worst sufferers were poor rural women. The government has launched social forestry programme which was supposed to benefit the poor but it has not done so. Poor rural women should be involved in social forestry by the government so that they are able to benefit. If they are organised and trained they will be able to participate better.[5]

Policies related to industry, handloom and handicrafts and home-based workers are all not very favourable to rural women. In industry when new technology is introduced women get displaced easily because they are unskilled. Women involved in handicrafts and other home based work do not get sufficient attention and face problems like low wages, difficulty in getting raw material and in marketing etc. The Credit Policy also favours big farmers and commercialisation of agriculture rather than poor women. Studies have shown that institutional fund flow does not encourage women's absorption into the mainstream of the economy. Thus we see that inspite of various schemes for rural women, they are not benefiting by them as much as they should, due to various reasons. A study in Tamil Nadu has shown that the benefits of IRDP have gone to educated, higher caste non-agricultural workers rather than to poor low caste agricultural workers. This is true about many other schemes. Overall evaluations by Government agencies as well as evaluations by independent researchers have also shown that the poorest of the poor have not benefited by the schemes for rural development, rather the rich farmers and other higher caste people have benefited more. The reason is that in our society the caste hierarchy affects life to a great extent and more so in villages where caste system is still strong.

In Uttaranhal vaious schemes are being implemented by the Government, for women, specially for empowerment of rural women. The Women's Empowerment and Child Development Dept. is running the Swashakti Pariyojna for providing training and employment to women, specially rural women. An ambitious initiative of the government towards empowerment of women is the Indira Mahila Samekit Vikas Yojna. Its objectives include gender sensitization and attitudinal change, increasing women's active participation in decision-making process at Panchayat level, developing skill and entrepreneurship among women, providing water and sanitation facilities for women, promoting legal literacy and leadership among women.

**Problems Faced by Rural Women :** As mentioned many times, inspite of so many schemes for rural development, the rural poor, both men and women are suffering in many ways. In fact most recent research work shows that the rural poor are actually going from bad to worse now a days. Abhijit Sen of JNU has studied the comsumption of the bottom 80% of the rural population and has found that for these people, numbering 600 million, consumption has actually declined in last 15 years. Their food intake has gone down resulting in malnutrition and poor health. Arun Firodia, after quoting Sen, writes that over 25,000 have committed suicide since 1997. While urban India is booming due to globalisation, the rural poor are dying. Of course women bear the brunt of all these problems because in our patriarchal setup women are given the least importance in all aspects of life, be it nutrition, health care or other facilities. Women have to work extra hard when men are unemployed or even commit suicide, to maintain the family and bring up the children. Many authors have spoken about 'feminisation of poverty' which means that in modern times women are more poor than men although they work more. Desai and Krishna Raj write that modern industrial economy has led to feminisation of poverty. The rural women have to travel longer distances to get water, fuel and fodder, due to extensive deforestation which wastes their time, their earnings are taken away by their husbands, they are paid very less in agricultural labour, and their traditional main occupation, the cottage industries have been displaced. All this has marginalised women in economy and led to feminisation of poverty. The authors refer to the studies of Majumdar and Gulati which conclude that in agriculture women have less control over resources, they are hardest hit due to landlessness. They have not only been bypassed by the development process but their traditional roles and status in society have been altered adversely by the nature of the development process itself. Another factor that places a heavy burden on women is male migration. Women have to fend for themselves and take care of the family. It was found that female headed households and poverty go together in villages.[6] All this applies to the rural women of Garhwal to a great extent. Specially the problems of deforestation and migration are very typical of the hills.

Authors from Garhwal like Rukma Rawat, Himanshu Borai, Ekta Unniyal and Sudesh Arya have written in detail about the problems faced by the hill women. Arya writes that quite often women meet with accidents while collecting water and fuel from far off places and carrying heavy loads on hilly tracts. Some of these accidents are fatal. Some times they are attacked by wild animals when they go to the forest to collect fodder and fuel. Borai writes about the social problems of hill women. In a patriarchal society they have no property rights if sons are present. If there are only daughters then they get some property but even that is handled by the husbands. Polygyny is still found and women have to put up with husbands' second wives. An old custom of deserting unwanted wives known as Choot Pratha is now very rare but earlier a man used to just announce that he is leaving his wife, in front of the Panchayat and left her. Some times she was bought by some other man. Rukma Rawat describes the various activities that rural women indulge in in Garhwal. Besides doing all housework they work in fields and take part in many community activities. Zainab Rahman writes that the role of rural, poor women is very tough. They bear the brunt of the struggle for survial. They not only work at home, but in fields, in forests, with the household animals and in cottage industries.

In the present study too, the researcher noticed that the rural women lead a very tough and busy life. If they are poor they have all the more problems, but even women who are not very poor have to work hard to do all household chores which include taking care of animals and collecting firewood and fodder. They have the minimum of facilities to do all this. Atleast they have a good water supply in most of the sample villages so they don't have to carry water from far away. We will discuss the other facilities in following chapters.

In this chapter we have discussed the ground realities of rural women in the sense that we have surveyed all the major schemes that are being implemented for them and also evaluated how far these schemes have helped the rural women. Next we have studied in detail the various problems that the rural women, specially in Garhwal, face in their day to day life. We will discuss all apects of their lives, the benefits that are available to them and also the hindrances in the improvement of their present condition in the following chapters.

## References

1. Laxmi Devi A 1987 Rural Women.
2. Verma & Nath 2004 Women and Rural Development Programmes.
3. Dhar SN 2005 Mocro Finance and Women.
4. Singh AK [2000] Empowerment of Women in India.
5. Verma & Nath 2004 Women and Rural Development Programmes.
6. Desai Krishna Raj Women and Society in India.

# 4

# Rural Women of Uttarakhand

Uttaranchal, the hill state in the north of the country, came into existence on 9th November 2000. It is the 27th State of the country. It comprises thirteen districts. The map of Uttaranchal presents the details. Dehradun, which is the biggest and most developed city is presently the capital of Uttaranchal. The local demand is that Gairsain should be made the permanent capital due to its central situation. It is a State rich in natural resources. It has abundant natural beauty and tourism is being developed as a major industry. Among its human resources, women form a big asset. The women of Uttaranchal are very hard working and are active not only in homes but in the fields, in community work and in socio-political movements. It is commonly said that women form the backbone of hill economy. The women of Uttarakhand are also known for their awareness and political acumen. They have taken initiative in famous movements like the Chipko Andolan, the Uttarakhand movement for a separate state and other socio-political movements like anti-liquor movement, anti-mining movement and afforestation and land reclamation processes. Although they play such an important role in society, they occupy a subordinate position in the patriarchal set up and face many hindrances and problems; yet it can be said that their status is slightly better than women in the plains and less restrictions are placed on their actions and movements. This may be because in the absence of men, most of these women have to shoulder all types of responsibilities and take various decisions on their own. The men are generally forced to migrate to other places to find employment. Men consider women as their 'Punji' [capital] because they do most of the work. The hill economy is sometimes also known as money order economy because of the fact that men live in far away places.

Writing about development in the new state of Uttaranchal, PN Pandey comments on the importance of women. He writes hill agriculture is dependent on women. The participation of women in economic and non-economic activities is considerably higher in the region as they remain busy in performing agricultural work and attending to cattle heads, collecting fuel, fodder and water and doing household chores. Women undoubtedly play an unenviable role in the socio-economic set up of the hill economy. They are over burdened with work, have a low status in society, have a low profile of their perception and outlook, suffer from poor health and lack of general awareness. Inspite of various development programmes aimed at uplift of women folk, no significant improvement can be observed in their life style. He suggests that while designing development policies, the planners should take into consideration the gender discrimination and inequality in access to resources that exists in our society. He also suggests that women should be given vocational training and encouraged to become economically independent so that their status improves and they take a step in the direction of empowerment. Handicraft activities based on natural resources and locally available raw material can provide easy opportunities of employment and income generation.[1] Here it may be mentioned that the State government has started various projects to encourage entrepreneurship and economic independence among hill women; for instance in Rourkee there is a scheme to organise local Muslim women to prepare agarbattis and Halwa for sale at the Dargah at Peeran Kalyar. There are many other schemes underfoot to make women economically independent and these will be discussed in detail later. Let us first take note of all the development plans and projects that were started for the women of this area since independence.

Before the formation of the State of Uttaranchal, which has recently been renamed Uttarakhand on demand of local people who fought for its formation, it was a part of Uttar Pradesh. The Uttarakhand area consists of two main sub regions, Kumaon and Garhwal, which are both hilly regions and the Terai and Bhabbar region which lies at the foothills and includes plains. Ever since independence, what ever schemes were started for rural development under the Community Development Programme, were implemented all over the State in a similar way. These programmes were mainly for improvement of agriculture, employment opportunities and for special target groups like landless labourers and small farmers, but there was no special plan for women. The Garhwal and Kumaon regions being hill areas, their conditions, problems and potentialities were quite different to the plains and the various schemes were not very suitable for them. Secondly some parts were very remote so the development schemes did not reach there. Due to these reasons these hilly areas remained backward and neglected. When it became evident to the Government that implementation of similar programmes in all parts of the country is not bearing expected results, the concept of regional planning was introduced. Regional planning basically assumes the concept of a region-a territorial space with varying interest and development prospects-as a unit of planning. Regional level planning is an essential tool of analysis and policy making to reconcile the conflicting claims of rural and urban development or the needs of achieving regional balance. It is mainly at this level that macro planning becomes coordinated and translated into project for implementation. This type of planning is becoming important because only through it can equalisation in social development and levels of living be possible. In a big country like India with lots of diversity and regional imbalances, regional planning is the only means of achieving the objective of balanced development.

In 1969, the Planning Commission stated that it has become apparent that plan formulation undertaken exclusively at the State level cannot possibly take into account, fully, the variety of condition existing in the different physio-geographical and economic regions of the states. Therefore resources should be provided and programmes taken up for particular areas or regions on the basis of specific and local assessment of their problems, reources and productive potential. It was only after this that specific programmes for the neglected hill areas of Uttar Pradesh were formulated and implemented keeping in mind the specific conditions, limitations and problems of hill people. Many studies have shown that in the first twenty five years of development planning in India, there was hardly any special programme for women, whether rural or urban because it was thought that the general progress made by the population as a whole would ultimately be shared by all sections, and benefits would accrue to both men and women. This assumption was proved wrong by the findings of CSWI which published its report, Towards Equality, in 1974, which concluded that women's status was unsatisfactory and they needed to be viewed as 'critical actors of development'; and not just as targets of welfare policies. Narasimhan writes that even after this, the planners' approach remained largely unchanged and by the end of the Fourth Five Year Plan it was clear that the growth effect was not trickling down to weaker sections including women. A minimum needs programme was there fore incorporated in the Fifth Plan, but there was no mention of women's specific needs in the areas listed for priority attention under the programme.[2]

The observance of an International Women's Year in 1975 resulted in attention being focused on women; their problems and needs, and in April 1975, the Lok Sabha passed a resolution to initiate comprehensive programmes for women. Rural women's development thus received priority for first time during the Sixth Plan period. In this way, we see that any specific plans for the rural women in Uttarakhand region started only in the late seventies Earlier the schemes were not area or person specific.

Under regional planning it was realised in the late seventies that there has been an alarming degradation and depletion of natural resources in hill areas, there fore stress was laid on 'development without destruction' strategy in formulating plans for hill areas. In other words, sustainable development was started. In the Seventh Plan an integrated approach based on systems analysis was introduced into the developmental planning for hills, taking into consideration the special socio-cultural and agro-ecological problems of those areas. The plan laid stress on the following points in hill areas: proper land use and soil and water conservation, massive afforestation, development of alternative sources of energy, development of micro-hydel energy, better employment facilities by encouraging resource based industries, suitable technical training and extension services for local needs and promoting industries with minimum pollution. In the year 1987-88 various recommendations were made by a high level meeting under the Chairmanship of the Minister of State for Planing, GOI., for improving hill areas and bringing about all round development. The various schemes for rural development which were implemented in the Sixth and Seventh plans in hill areas included IRDP, DPAP, IREP and NREP. Besides there were programmes for weaker sections including SC ST and bonded labourers. There were programmes for applied nutrition for pregnant and lactating mothers, special nutrition for children between 0-6 years of age and mid day meal programme for children between 6-11 years of age. In the 70s the Antyodaya Programme was implemented by the Janata Government to help the porest of the poor families in villages but was not very successful.

In her book 'Daughters of the Earth, Women and Land in Uttar Pradesh', Smita Tewari Jassal writes that women are denied property rights and in modern times they are losing control over natural resources to a greater extent due to shift from communal ownership of resources to increasing privatisation. In 1981 a survey of bonded labour in UP showed that 10.40 per cent of agricultural labour is still bonded and of these 74 per cent belong to the Scheduled Castes. When men are bonded their women folk suffer all types of exploitation.[3]

In the second half of the Sixth Five Year Plan a special programme for rural women namely DWCRA was started. Beginning with 50 districts, this revolving grant scheme had by the end of the Eighth Plan, covered 291 districts. With the central and state governments and UNICEF, each contributing one-third of the seed money, the women beneficiaries were encouraged to form thrift groups. The women were also provided various types of vocational training at community centres. This programme was quite successful till UNICEF was involved, later it lost some of its dynamism, due to resource crunch, inspite of networking by women. In the 80s and 90s various rural dvelopment programmes were implemented under IRDP. Besides DWCRA which was specially for women, there were other programmes like TRYSEM, RLEGP and FFWP and Skill Development Programme which were meant to help rural population learn skills and get employment. Another scheme for women was the Support for Employment of Women Programme, STEP launched by the Department of Women and Child Development GOI. A new Employment Guarantee Scheme, through Shram Shakti [voluntary community labour] was introduced specifically for women belonging to the SC/STs below the poverty line as a priority group, but it calls for atleast 50 workers to make themselves available every day as a binding condition in the absence of which there is no guarantee of work. This is one example of the insensitivity of planners to the problems of poor rural women. In the 90s various other schemes for rural women were started namely, Mahila Samriddhi Yogna, Indira Mahila Yojna, setting up of National Commission for Women in 1991 and Rashtriya Mahila Kosh in 1993 and reservation of 33% seats in election to local bodies in 1994 through the 73 rd Constitutional Amendment. But in spite of all these, the status of women is not yet fully satisfactory due to various socio-cultural reasons as well as lack of political will. Narasimhan writes in her book, Empowering Women, ' at the end of each plan period, it has been conceded by the drafters of the succeeding Plan document, that the projects of the foregoing period did not deliver results commensurate with the effort or the need of the target groups. This repeated acknowledgement notwithstanding, no alternative methods or strategies seem to have been thought of, much less explored.' She writes that the NGOs on the other hand have helped rural women to a great extent in improving their lot and gives a detailed account of the work of AWARE, in southern states. Here the author would like to present a Table from her book which shows the dismal position of Uttar Pradesh among major states of India in Human development and Gender Development Indices.

**Table : Human Development Index and Gender Development Index in major states of India**

| *Name* | *Life expectancy* | *literacy -91* | *HDI 91-92* | *GDI 91-92* |
|---|---|---|---|---|
| Kerala | 72 | 90 | 0.603 | 0.565 |
| Punjab | 66.4 | 59 | 0.529 | 0.424 |
| Maharashtra | 64.2 | 65 | 0.523 | 0.492 |
| Haryana | 62.9 | 56 | 0.489 | 0.37 |
| Gujarat | 60.1 | 61 | 0.467 | 0.437 |
| West Bengal | 61.5 | 58 | 0.459 | 0.399 |
| Himachal Pradesh | 63.6 | 64 | 0.454 | 0.432 |
| Karnataka | 61.9 | 56 | 0.448 | 0.417 |
| Tamil Nadu | 62.4 | 63 | 0.438 | 0.402 |
| Andhra Pradesh | 60.6 | 44 | 0.4 | 0.371 |
| Assam | 54.9 | 53 | 0.379 | 0.347 |
| Orissa | 55.5 | 49 | 0.373 | 0.329 |
| Rajasthan | 58 | 39 | 0.356 | 0.309 |
| Bihar | 58.5 | 38 | 0.354 | 0.306 |
| Madhya Pradesh | 54 | 44 | 0.349 | 0.312 |
| Uttar Pradesh | 55.9 | 42 | 0.348 | 0.293 |
| INDIA | 59.4 | 52 | 0.425 | 0.388 |

*Source* : India : The Road to Human Development UNDP p. 47. States are ranked in descending order of HDI. A GDI of 1.0 represents equality between men and women, figures lower than 1.0 indicate the extent of disparityas per measures devised by the UNDP Human Development Report 1995. Delhi 1997.

This table shows that the performance of Uttar Pradesh was very dismal till early 90s. both in HDI and GDI.

Steps being taken for empowerment of women in the Ninth and Tenth Plans are discussed in great detail elsewhere. In this regard various national schemes for women's development were also implemented in Uttar Pradesh.

In Uttaranchal, various schemes and programmes for empowerment of women have been implemented and women are making progress in most fields, specially in the areas of political participation and employment. Some important schemes include Swa Shakti Yojna, Swayam Siddha Yojna, Kishori Shakti Yojna and Balika Samriddhi Yojna. The Watershed Management Programme was implemented in the hill areas of UP in the 90s. It is still being implemented in rural Uttaranchal for integrated rural development, under the name of IWDP [Integrated Watershed Development Project] . At present an ambitious initiative of Government of Uttaranchal towards Women Empowerment is the Indira Mahila Samekit Vikas Yojna. Its vision is to build such empowered women who will participate in decision making processs for effective contribution towards social, economic and political development. Its mission is to provide financial assistance to Project Proposals for meeting the special needs of mountain women as well as to address various aspects of women's empowerment. Its mandatory objectives include gender sensitisation and attitudinal change, plantation of fodder grasses and fuel species on community land to reduce drudgery of routine work, promotion of non conventional energy sources, water and sanitation facilities for rural women, enhancement of women's active participation in decision making process in Panchayati Raj institutions. It also aims to create women specific infrastructure and offer them opportunities for employment, develop women friendly technologies and create awareness and legal literacy. This programme has made the following achievements to date : Financial asistance to viable project proposals, initiation of interventions for drudgery reduction and empowerment of 7265 women beneficiaries till 31st December 2005. These include plantation of fodder grass and wormi-composting, demonstration of wheat thrashers and rice dehuskers, establishment of collection center and fruit processing units capacity building programme and micro enterprise development.[4]

Despite the fact that the hill areas of Uttar Pradesh were neglected and economically backward, rural women in these areas have always been very active in socio-economic sphere of community life. Women of Garhwal and Kumaon have a long history of struggle against authorities for various causes like preventing deforestation, mining activity or alcoholism among men. They have taken initiative in anti alcoholism drive. They have always played a prominent and critical role in environmental conservation and forest management. The leadership role they played in the world famous Chipko Movement is well known. The names of Gaura Devi and Bala Devi are now legends. The women of the Chipko movement were awarded the Right Livelihood award in 1987 instituted for vision and work contributing to making life more whole, healing our planet and uplifting humanity. It was given to the Chipko Andolan women for putting life of forests above their own. Chandi Prasad Bhatt, the Magsaysay Award winner, notes that women in the hilly and tribal regions are the best protectors of environment, specially forests as they are the worst sufferers from their destruction. Providing daily household needs of fodder, fuel and water is primarily the responsibility of these women but their job has become increasingly difficult in the face of systematic loss of forests That is one of the reasons why the women of the hill state of Uttarakhand played such an active role in the Chipko movement launched in the 70s to prevent felling of trees.[5] Even today the women are involved in conservation of the environment by taking part in afforestation drives. A key input in the afforestation programme has been the organization of women's groups, which have tried to secure the common lands for firewood and fodder production. They have also attempted to distribute the available firewood and grass equitably. Besides afforestation the volunteers have taken up appropriate soil conservation measures in heavily eroded landscapes like planting fast growing grass, by plugging gullies and building small check dams. They have also promoted energy saving devices like bio gas plants and fuel efficient stoves.[6] Dr. Zainab Rahman quotes Dr Rukma Rawat in her book, Women and Society, describing the work of rural Garhwali women. She writes, These women become heads of the families in the absence of men and take various decisions in the family and also work as peasants. Besides this, they take an active interest in community matter. In every village there is an informal female organization known as the Mahila Panchayat, which takes up activities like guarding the community forests, opening of the fields for weeding, cutting grass, harvesting and cutting branches from community forests for their needs, distributing water among villagers when there is acute shortage of water and organizing the worship of community deity. Women of the Mahila Mangal Dal of Falayanti village in Bageshwar district under took to accomplish a unique afforestation project on 25 ha of degraded land in their village. They were locally coordinated by Diksha Bisht who has been conferred the Meiti Award by Jalagam. The project received aid from National Afforestation and Eco-Development Board, but it was totally a women's project. They have converted pine monoculture into mixed forest and today, broad-leaved species of ecological, fodder, food and fuel value, numbering 130,000 are flourishing in the area. The local Van Panchayat has taken the responsibility of maintaining thc plantation.[7]

Women of Uttarakhand have always been active in politics. Some women participated in the 1942 Quit India Movement and also in Satyagraha movement. Names like Kunti Devi, Tulsi Devi Rawat and Durgawati Pant are worth mentioning. In the recent Uttarakhand Andolan, for a separate hill state, women played a leading and crucial role. In fact it was the women who kept the movement alive in different parts of the state. They participated fully in all forms of protests like dharnas, rallies, fasts and strikes. At Rampur Tiraha, women were molested and some lost their lives, still the women of Uttarakhand continued with their struggle and achieved success finally.[8] Women have become active in village politics since the reservation of 33 per cent seats for them in local bodies' elections. In Uttarakhand women Pradhans and Panchayat members have been quite successful in working efficiently for the welfare of their villages. Many NGOs are also helping rural women to perform their duties as Panchayat member efficiently. Panchayati Raj in Uttaranchal has given an opportunity to ordinary women to interact with the administration on a daily basis and carry on development work in their areas. PRAGATI, headed by Ruchi Kukreti under the aegis of the well known NGO, RLEK, has been working consistently for the past eight years to make rural women representatives of the Panchayats in the hill state aware of their strength and to ensure that the information needed by them is constantly updated. In June 2006 the women representatives of Panchayati Raj from Pauri and Hardwar districts gathered in Kotdwar for a two day open forum and passed the Pauri Declaration in which they have called upon the Uttaranchal government to immediately pass the Uttaranchal Panchayati Raj Act. They also complained that the state politicians and bureaucrats were creating obstacles in the functioning of Panchayati raj members. They also demanded access to and control over natural resources on which their livelihood depends. They demanded an enquiry into the distribution of land in Uttaranchal to outsiders. These women have been trained and sensitized by PRAGATI functionaries. This is an example of the awareness and initiative level of women of Uttarakhand.[9]

All these instances of the courage, perseverance and hard work of hill women prove that they have a great potential to make progress. Given proper support in the form of training and knowledge, they will achieve much more than what they have done already.

In the new state the women are being encouraged in various ways to improve their lot and get empowered. The various programmes were mentioned above. The Women Empowerment and Child development Department in the Uttaranchal government was running the Swashakti Pariyojna aided by World Bank and IFAD. This project was implemented in 14 development blocks of Tehri, Almora and Pithoragarh districts and was completed in March 2005. It trained the women to become economically independent and formed self help groups. Efforts are on to continue the good work and encourage more and more women to learn about various schemes for their development and benefit through them. At present a number of schemes for vocational training, employment, entrepreneurship and access to facilities are being implemented by different departments like Rural Development Dept., Social welfare dept., Cooperative Dept., Tourism Depart, Agriculture and Animal Husbandry Depts. and of course the Women's Empowerment and Child Development Depart. for rural population in general and rural women in particular.[10]

The NGOs are also doing exemplary work in empowering women We have already mentioned the work being done by RLEK and PRAGATI to educate rural women about their rights and their roles as Panchayat members. Many other NGOs like SAMARPIT, DISHA, KOHISH and HESCO are working with rural women to empower them. Dr Anil Joshi of HESCO has done pioneering work in using indigenous technology to help farmers. The author will now present some of the details of various activities of women of Uttarakhand that are enabling them to improve their own lives and those of their family members. The Maiti movement of Uttaranchal was first introduced in a small village of Garhwal by Kalyan Singh Rawat, a Zoology teacher who wanted women and girls to get involved in environmental conservation in an organized way. He was inspired by the fact that girl students took keen interest in nature and he also was aware of women's role in the Chipko Andolan. The mass appeal of Maiti has made its presence felt in even remote villages and within four years it had spread to all parts of the state. Maiti means parental home in Garhwali and the word has perfectly blended emotional factors with a strong feeling for eco-conservation. This is a women centric movement. In this a few young girls form a Maiti group and choose a leader, Maiti Didi. The group prepares a Maiti nursery in the village or town. On the day of the wedding of a member, a sapling is brought in front of the bride and groom and the bride gives it to the groom who plants it in the bride's parental home. The groom contributes some money to Maiti volunteers. The money thus collected is used for needy girls. It also contributes to the marriages of poor girls. The sapling is taken care of by the parents. Thus Maiti is not just a carrier of emotions but also protector of ecology and culture. The women folk in the remote Ochati village developed a sprawling Maiti forest in the memory of the martyrs of Kargil. The ritual of planting saplings at birthdays, anniversaries etc. is catching on fast in the state.[11]

Eco tourism and Community based tourism is another strategy which is aimed at promoting the Tourism industry in a sustainable way and also benefiting the local people by involving them in it. The scheme for Muslim women of Rourkee, mentioned earlier is an example. Recently village communities in and around Corbett Tiger Reserve have been roped in to be part of eco-tourism in Uttaranchal, helping them earn a livelihood. A fascinating Jim Corbett Heritage Trail has been developed as a part of Uttaranchal's keen effort to promote community based tourism [CBT] in Chhoti Haldwani village in Kaladhungi, about 30 km from Corbett Tiger Reerve. The CBT Project members guide visitors along this trail, run a souvenir shop, have home stays in two families, maintain an information kiosk and have recently started tours for areas adjoining Kaladhungi. Another attractive and informative CBT project is 'The Chipko Heritage Trail'developed in Reni village on the outskirts of the Nanda Devi National Park. The trail takes visitors to the fir forests where the residents of Reni village first embraced fir trees under the leadership of Gaura Devi, marking the beginning of Chipko movement in the 70s.[12]

Another initiative for the hill women is the setting up of 24 hour free Help line for Women in Distress, in May 2004. The main purpose is to provide advisory support and relief to the callers undergoing emotional distress or depression arising out of their typical personal or social predicaments. The need for such a helpline arose from the sudden upsurge in cases of suicide and violence against women.

The Uttranchal State Commission for Women has also been set up to prevent all types of exploitation and discrimination against women, to fight for their constitutional rights and to increase their legal and general awareness. It also coordinates the welfare work of various departments to contribute to women's development.

After presenting information about the women of Uttarakhand in general, we now come to the present study which is an evaluation of the level of empowerment of rural women living in ten villages in Garhwal area of the state. The following chapters give the details of the study, and the major conclusions reached after analysis of data.

## References

1. Ekta Unniyal 2003 The Study of Uttaranchal Mentor Publications.
2. Narsimhan 1999 Empowering Women age Publications.
3. Jassal S T 2001 Daughters of the Earth Manohar.

4. Asha 2005 Brochure on IMSVY Published by Women Empowerment and Child Development Depart. Uttaranchal Govt.
5. News in Hindustan Times HT 26th March 2007.
6. Sumi Krishna 1996 Environmental Politics Sage.
7. News Item in Times of India TOI 2nd Oct.2004.
8. Rahman Zainab 2005 Women and Society Kalpaz.
9. News Item in Times of India TOI 1st May and 3rd June 2006.
10. Asha 2005 Publication of Women Empowerment and Child Development Depart. Uttaranchal Govt.
11. Ekta Uniyal 2003 The Study of Uttaranchal Mentor Publications.
12. News Item in Times of India TOI–Doon Plus 11th March 2007.

# 5

# Socio Economic Status of the Respondents

The poor in India are overwhelmingly concentrated in the villages and are engaged in agriculture and related occupations. They follow some non-agricultural occupations too. These workers are mostly wage labourers, self employed petty labourers and artisans. They belong to the backward, unorganized and deprived sections of the work force. Even though there have been signs of improvement in the standard of living, the rural labour has been largely bypassed by the process of socio-economic development over the last five decades.[1] In the present study too the researcher noticed poverty and backwardness in some parts of the sample villages. These areas were inhabited by the poorest of the poor in the village, but many others seem to have a comfortable standard of living. The socio-economic status of a person or group can be evaluated in terms of that person or group's gender, religion, caste, income, education, occupation and place of habitation. All these factors or variables decide the position of a person or a group in the society and also influence that person or group's behaviour and attitudes.

This chapter will give a detailed description of the various aspects of the lives of the respondents like their age, their education, income, religion and caste and details of their family. All these variables are very important in studying the behaviour and attitudes of people because they have a direct influence on them. Old people may react differently to the same situation than younger people, due to the change in experience, similarly educated people have different attitudes than uneducated people due to their knowledge.

In the present sample 200 rural women of different ages, education, income group and religion etc., were interviewed to collect primary data for the research. Besides questions about their social and economic variables, they were also asked questions to find out about the level of their economic independence, their decision making power, their access to basic facilities and their political participation. Questions were also asked to find out their attitudes towards some important issues related to women as well as their level of awareness. This would show what positive changes have taken place in their mental makeup. They were also asked about the various difficulties they have to face in the village, with a view to evaluate their condition and also to suggest solutions to the problems.

The data regarding the socio-economic status of the respondents is being presented in two columns, column 'a' for respondents from villages of Raipur block and column 'b' for respondents from the villages in Doiwala block. Table No.1 presents the age wise distribution of the respondents.

**Table 1 : Distribution of Respondents by their Age**

| *S.No.* | *Categories* | *No. of Respondents 'a'* | *No. of Respondents 'b'* | *Percent* |
|---|---|---|---|---|
| 1. | less than 20yrs | 3 | 3 | 3 |
| 2. | 21–30 yrs | 32 | 39 | 35.5 |
| 3. | 31-40 | 38 | 27 | 32.5 |
| 4. | 41-50 | 17 | 21 | 19 |
| 5. | 51–60 | 10 | 9 | 9.5 |
| 6. | above 60 yrs | 0 | 1 | .5 |
| | Total | 100 | 100 | 100 |

As seen in the table the maximum number of women are between the ages of 20 to 40 years, which are the most productive years. The next big group is of women between 41 to 60 years of age who are mostly the older generation with married children. Thus we had women of two generations in our sample with children of varying ages. There were some differences in their thinking specially with regard to importance of education and need for women to be economically independent. The older onces too agreed that education and personal income are important now, but they were more resigned to their condition whereas the younger ones wanted to earn and see to it that their daughters get better education. Some old women were however, quite independent and active and worked for their living. The younger women were more aware and were in favour of women's equality whereas the older ones did not have much faith in equality. All this shows that with time, even in the villages, women are becoming more aware of the injustice done to them by our society and are trying to attain their rightful position.

Education is a very important variable as it increases the knowledge of a person and makes him more broad minded and logical. Table 2 presents the details of the educational levels of the respondents.

**Table 2 : Distribution of Respondents by their Education**

| S.No. | Categories | No. of Respondents 'a' | No. of Respondents 'b' | Percent |
|---|---|---|---|---|
| 1. | Uneducated | 41 | 56 | 48.5 |
| 2. | Primary School | 24 | 9 | 16.5 |
| 3. | Middle School | 10 | 10 | 10 |
| 4. | High School | 12 | 17 | 14.5 |
| 5. | College | 13 | 8 | 10.5 |
| | Total | 100 | 100 | 100 |

It is sad to note that nearly half the women in the sample are uneducated, specially because Dehradun district has the highest female literacy rate [71.22%] in the State. This shows that the gap between rural and urban rates is quite big. Still, as compared to other rural women elsewhere in the country, a literacy rate of 51.5% is good because many studies have noted that illiteracy rate among rural women in some cases is as high as 90%. It is heartening that one fourth of the respondents have passed high school and 10.5% are college educated. For this the nearby cities, specially Dehradun are responsible. In the oldest PG College for girls in Dehradun a lot of students come from nearby villages. Many respondents said their daughters studied in this college [MKP PG College] and some of them had also studied there themselves. Now of course Inter colleges for girls are found in some of the sample villages and there are also colleges for higher and professional education near Hansuwala and Bhaniyawala. There are Government schools in almost all villages and many villages also have Private English medium schools. Some parents send their children to schools in Dehradun, specially from Ajabpur Kalan and Ajabpur Khurd. There is an intellectual and educational ambiance in Dehradun and female education is also encouraged fully, hence we see its effect on the sample too.

Table 3 gives the details of the income groups to which the respondents belong. Income is a very important variable which affects all aspects of life and is of great importance in today's materialistic world.

**Table 3 : Distribution of Respondents by their Family Income**

| *S.No.* | *Categories* | *No. of Respondents 'a'* | *No. of Respondents 'b'* | *Percent* |
|---|---|---|---|---|
| 1. | less than Rs 1000 | 17 | 16 | 16.5 |
| 2. | Rs 1001–Rs 2000 | 33 | 44 | 38.5 |
| 3 | Rs 2001–Rs 3000 | 18 | 26 | 22 |
| 4 | Rs 3001–Rs 4000 | 6 | 6 | 6 |
| 5. | Rs 4001–Rs 5000 | 20 | 4 | 12 |
| 6. | Rs 5001 and above | 6 | 4 | 5 |
| | Total | 100 | 100 | 100 |

The data show that 16.5 per cent respondents live below poverty line while a majority of them are quite poor. Only 5 per cent respondents have an income above Rs 5000 per month. Another 18 per cent are among lower middle class. Income plays a very important role in developing concepts and attitudes and in influencing behaviour. Poor people may like to do many things but cannot due to economic restraints. For instance many poor parents are not able to provide education to children, specially girls, because they are needed at home when the mother goes out to work as a labourer. This does not mean that they do not want to educate their daughters or that they look down upon girls. In the present sample only a few respondents said that their children do not go to school while an overwhelming majority sends both sons and daughters to school and college, even if they are poor. Income also affects consumption patterns and life style. In the present sample the poor respondents had a low standard of living, the poorest of the poor living in a small thatched room without proper kitchen or bathroom. Most respondents had a satisfactory standard of living in that they had the minimum basic facilities and a 'pucca' house.

Religion is a factor which influences the beliefs and attitudes of people. In India people of different religions live together and generally have harmonious relations. The secular atmosphere of our society encourages this harmony. In the present sample too, peaceful co-existance was noticed. Table 4 presents the distribution of respondents by religion.

**Table 4 : Distribution of Respondents by their Religion**

| *S.No.* | *Categories* | *No. of Respondents 'a'* | *No. of Respondents 'b'* | *Percent* |
|---|---|---|---|---|
| 1. | Hindu | 77 | 78 | 77.5 |
| 2 | Muslim | 20 | 22 | 21 |
| 3 | Sikh | 3 | 0 | 1.5 |
| | Total | 100 | 100 | 100 |

The data about religious distribution is very predictable, with an overwhelming majority of Hindus. The percentage of Muslims is higher than the national percentage because some villages have a big Muslim population like Ajabpur Kalan, Hansuwala and Bhaniyawala. Among the Muslims the high castes were less and the OBCs were more, but exact numbers are not being given because theoretically Muslims don't believe in caste system and some respondents didn't want to give any caste name. The Hindus were divided into different castes and communities and the details are given in the next table.

**Table 5 : Distribution of Hindu Respondents by Caste/ Community**

| *S.No.* | *Categories* | *No. of Respondents 'a'* | *No. of Respondents 'b'* |
|---|---|---|---|
| 1. | High castes | 12 | 13 |
| 2. | Nepali | 20 | 0 |
| 3. | Garhwali | 9 | 8 |
| 4 | Bihari | 0 | 4 |
| 5. | OBCs | 21 | 23 |
| 6. | Sch. Caste | 15 | 30 |
| | Total | 77 | 78 |

As seen in the table some respondents gave their caste and some their community hence they have been differentiated as such. There are no OBCs in Garhwalis so practically all belong to high castes, mainly Brahmin and Rajput. The bulk of Hindus were of OBCs and Scheduled castes, who were quite poor. Nepalis live in Ajabpur and Navada and are quite prosperous and politically active. Biharis were found in Doiwala villages and are poor. Among the high caste Hindus there were Brahmins, Rajputs and Baniyas. An important phenomenon noticed in all villages was communal harmony. Details of this will be given in later chapters. All castes and creeds coexist peacefully and work together in these villages.

Rural occupations are different from urban occupations. The main occupation in villages are agriculture and related occupations, animal husbandry and cottage industries. Today, the farmers are facing many hardships, specially the small farmers. Many of them are forced to sell their land or forfeit it to money lenders due to abject poverty and indebtedness. Thus the number of small cultivators is decreasing and number of agricultural labourers is increasing. These labourers are very poor because they are forced to work for low wages and have no bargaining power. Most rural women are labourers or self employed workers. They belong to the non-institutionalised unorganized sector.[2] These women are forced to work in these occupations due to poverty. They face problems of low wages, lack of job security, exploitation and sexual harassment. Studies on women in informal sector highlight that women predominate in the informal sector and they are concentrated in a narrow range of activities with lowest returns. These studies conclude that poverty and gender restrictions make women accept any work on any terms either at home or outside.[3] The tables below present the details of family occupation and personal occupation of respondents.

**Table 6 : Distribution of Respondents by Family Occupation**

| *S.No.* | *Categories* | *No. of Respondents 'a'* | *No. of Respondents 'b'* | *Percent* |
|---|---|---|---|---|
| 1. | Farming | 15 | 23 | 19 |
| 2. | Agri. Labour | 6 | 8 | 7 |
| 3. | Animal Husbandry | 6 | 10 | 8 |

| | | | | |
|---|---|---|---|---|
| 4 | Cottage industry | 25 | 32 | 28.5 |
| 5. | Service | 31 | 16 | 23.5 |
| 6. | Business | 10 | 7 | 8.5 |
| 7 | Any other | 7 | 4 | 5.5 |
| | Total | 100 | 100 | 100 |

**Table 7 : Distribution of Respondents by their Own Occupation**

| *S.No.* | *Categories* | *No. of Respondents 'a'* | *No. of Respondents 'b'* | *Percent* |
|---|---|---|---|---|
| 1. | Housewife | 70 | 70 | 70 |
| 2. | Labourer | 23 | 24 | 23.5 |
| 3. | Business | 4 | 3 | 3.5 |
| 4. | Teacher | 3 | 3 | 3 |
| | Total | 100 | 100 | 100 |

The first table shows that 26% respondents said their family occupation is based on agriculture, 8% said it is based on animal husbandry and 28.5% said it is based on cottage industries. Thus 62.5% respondents have purely rural occupations while the others are involved in service, which may be government job or private job and business of various kinds. The second table shows that a great majority of women are housewives only, which is quite natural. These housewives do a lot of productive work by helping in family occupation be it farming, cottage industry or animal husbandry. Besides they work on their own in many ways to make some money like stitching or working part time as domestic help or selling pickles etc. Thus although they are just housewives their contribution to village as well as family economy is considerable. They also provide economic help by collecting fodder and fuel for use at home. Nearly a fourth of the respondents work as full time agricultural labourers to earn money. These are the really poor women. Some of them are the heads of their household. A minute number is occupied as business woman and teacher. The researcher noticed that in the villages in Raipur block which are closer to Dehradun lesser men were dependent on agriculture and a greater number was of service class; whereas in the villages falling in Doiwala block, which are further away and appear more rural, greater number of men are involved in agriculture and animal husbandry. The number of male agricultural labourers is also greater in these villages. The number of female agricultural labourers is more or less the same in both blocks. They work out of necessity because they need money to survive and care for their families. Among cottage industries people are involved in weaving, basket and net making, carpentry, pottery and tailoring. The researcher noticed a couple of beauty parlours in Navada. The girls who work in them have got training from Dehradun but would like to have a training centre in the village too. One Nepali woman ran a general store in Navada. In the schools in the villages, a few teachers are from the village itself while most come from nearby towns. Women who work as Aanganwadi helpers and members of Panchayat and other groups have given their occupation as housewives because they work only part time. One respondent is running her own school in Majri Grant with the help of her husband; she has been classified as teacher.

After personal details we come to family details, because for rural women the family is very important and it controls them to a great extent. In our patriarchal society women are always given a lower status and lag behind in all development indicators. This is more pronounced in villages. Violence against women, which has its roots in the subordination of women at the social level is rampant in rural families and the wives accept it as a necessary evil.[4] Women are controlled by their husbands and other family members who restrict their outdoor activities. In the present sample too women agreed that they are controlled by their men, but mostly, they were allowed to take part in political activity as well as work outside home to earn money because this is helpful in running the household. In the sample 58.5% respondents live in joint families and 41.5% respondents live in nuclear families. The table below gives the details of family size.

**Table 8 : Distribution of Respondents by the Size of their Family**

| *S.No.* | *Categories* | *No. of Respondents 'a'* | *No. of Respondents 'b'* | *Percent* |
|---|---|---|---|---|
| 1. | 0-3 members | 7 | 9 | 8 |
| 2. | 4-6 members | 57 | 52 | 54.5 |
| 3. | 7-10 members | 30 | 36 | 33 |
| 4. | more than 10 members | 6 | 3 | 4.5 |
| | Total | 100 | 100 | 100 |

More than half the respondents have medium sized families which is a good sign from the population point of view. There are 8% small families too. One third families are big in size. The very big ones are bigger joint families which are made up of three nuclear families or so. It can be concluded then that in general the family size is satisfactory in the sample from the development point of view.

Children are an important part of the family. Generally rural families have a lot of children, mainly because villagers feel more children means more hands to work and secondly because they are ignorant about importance and means of family planning. But in modern times even villagers have learnt the importance of family planning and try to have less children whom they can educate and bring up well. The next table shows the details of number of children that the respondents have.

**Table 9 : Distribution of Respondents by the Number of their Children**

| S.No. | Categories | No. of Respondents 'a' | No. of Respondents 'b' | Percent |
|---|---|---|---|---|
| 1. | No children | 1 | 5 | 3 |
| 2. | 1-3 children | 66 | 52 | 59 |
| 3. | 4-6 children | 27 | 31 | 29 |
| 4. | 7-10 children | 6 | 12 | 9 |
| | Total | 100 | 100 | 100 |

As mentioned above, today even villagers understand ıe importance of having less children. A majority of the ›spondents i.e., 59% of them have 1–3 children and only % have a lot of children. A sizable number of them [29%] ıve 4–6 children which is not too big a number in villages. ıis shows that the sample has some knowledge of family ınning and its importance. The next table shows the details education of children.

**Table 10 : Distribution of Respondents by their Children's Education**

| ;.No. | Categories | No. of Respondents 'a' | No. of Respondents 'b' | Percent |
|---|---|---|---|---|
| | Children go to school | 89 | 81 | 85 |
| | Children do not go | 8 | 5 | 6.5 |

| | | | | |
|---|---|---|---|---|
| 3. | No children | 1 | 5 | 3 |
| 4. | Children grown up | 2 | 9 | 5.5 |
| | Total | 100 | 100 | 100 |

In today's world education of children is most important. The table shows that the respondents in the present study give importance to their children's education and only 6.5% said that their children do not go to school, 3% do not have children and 5.5% have grown up children. All the rest i.e., 85% respondents said their children, both sons and daughters, attend school or college. Approximately 70% said their children study in Government schools which have Hindi as medium of instruction. Nearly 30% send their children to private English medium schools. On being questioned about the level of education, nearly 80% said their children were in school, about 4% said they were in college and 1% said they were doing professional course.

The next information sought in the discussion of socio-economic status was the type of house the respondents live in. A huge majority, 91% of the respondents own their houses and only 9% live in rented houses. Again a large number of them, 77.5% have brick houses which are known as 'pucca' houses and 22.5% have mud huts with thatched roofs, known as "kaccha' houses. A good ventilated, hygienic home adds not only to comfort but also health and well being. Having one's own house, however small, is also a blessing and gives mental peace. The researcher noticed that many houses, both 'pucca' and 'kaccha' were not properly ventilated although nearly all had an open space in front of the house which they kept quite clean. Many families did not have proper kitchens or bathrooms. Other facilities available to the respondents are discussed in later chapters.

Thus the data about socio-economic status of respondents show that the sample is a composite group with rural women belonging to different religions, castes, age groups, educational levels and income groups. This signifies that the sample is quite representative of the universe, since our rural society has people of different strata, religion and caste. This also ensures that the researcher will be able to collect all shades of opinions and attitudes towards any particular phenomenon which exist in the sample.

In short we can conclude that the sample includes a majority of women in the age group of 21-40 years, 51.5% respondents are literate, with 25% having passed high school. Most of them belong to lower middle class, live in their own homes and have medium sized families.59% respondents have 1–3 children and 85% said their children are getting educated, only 6.5% said their children do not go to school. This shows that the respondents give importance to education of children although many of them are poor and uneducated themselves. With regard to occupation 62.5% respondents said their family occupation was of rural nature, 23.5% said their family occupation was based on service. The respondents themselves were overwhelmingly just housewives [70%] while 23.5% worked as agricultural labourers. As mentioned above the housewives contribute in many ways to the economy besides doing all the housework. They belonged to different religions and castes, majority being Hindus. Among the castes the OBCs and Scheduled Castes were greatest in number.

In the following chapters, other data related to the four variables under study will be presented systematically and in greater detail.

## References

1. Balakrishnan A 2005 Rural Landless Women Labourers, Kalpaz Publications.
2. Balakrishnan A 2005 Rural Landless Women Labourers, Kalpaz Publications.
3. Lingam Lakshmi 2006 Gender, Household and Poverty EPW, May 20th 2006.
4. Narasimhan S 1999 Empowering Women, Sage Publications.

# 6

# Rural Women and Political Participation

In her Foreword to the book, 'Empowering Women', Mohini Giri, former Chairperson of National Commission for Women, writes, 'We are on the threshold of the 21st century. During the past half a century, India has witnessed a positive transformation in women's empowerment and economic development while retaining a great diversity in its political and social system. Although India still has to go a long way in attaining gender equality and gender justice, no one can deny that its efforts towards redressing gender inequality are more pronounced than in many other countries. Gender justice should also include consideration of differential access to power, resources and opportunities, as well as autonomy of action and self and social valuation.'[1] It is true that efforts are on to empower women, specially the poor low caste rural women, but they are still highly exploited and oppressed in many ways. Money alone cannot improve their lot. Their powerlessness is not due to lack of money alone. It is due to the socio-cultural norms which do not allow them independence of any sort. One means of obtaining power is to have a say in the administration and decision making process of the community, i.e., to participate in politics. Political participation of women is quite low all over the world because politics is generally considered a male occupation, since it pertains to public life and women are expected to be confined to domestic life. Still in the modern world women have started participating in politics.

The political status of women in a nation is reflected by the extent of freedom granted to women with regard to their participation in the political activity. Political participation, according to Sydney Verba refers to acts by those not formally empowered to make decisions—the acts being intended to influence the behaviour of those who had such powers. 'Yet, successful participation refers to those acts that have [at least in part] the intended effects.' In a conventional analysis, political participation means voting, attending party meetings, campaigning, supporting pressure groups, active membership of political parties, holding party offices, contesting elections, raising party funds and communicating directly with legislators. All these activities are designed to influence decision making.[2] Haralambos presents Lester Milbrath's classification of political participation in his book. Milbrath has suggested that members of society can be divided into four categories in terms of their degree of political participation:

1. Those who are politically apathetic, i.e., those who do not know about the political world around them,

2. Those involved in spectator activities like voting and discussing politics,

3. Those involved in transitional activities like attending political meetings and contributing to political party funds,

4. Those who enter political arena and engage in gladiatorial activities like standing for and holding party offices.[3]

Feminist writers, Krishna Raj and Desai also refer to this model of hierarchy of political participation and comment that women in India are concerned more with spectator activity, little with transitional activity and very little with gladiatorial activity. It is not unusual for them to be apathetic.[4]

In India women were given equal rights in the Constitution and got the right to vote and fight elections, right from the time of the First General Elections, but the number of women active in politics has always been small and confined mostly to women of elite families with a political background. Although women form nearly half the population they are not considered as a powerful vote bank because generally women vote as ordered by their men and not as a block. In rural areas women used to be more apathetic earlier, but since the 73rd amendment to the Constitution in 1993, rural women have started participating actively in politics. This amendment was made on the demands of women's organizations in their report, Shram Shakti in 1988. According to this amendment which was adopted by the states in 1994, there is provision of one–third reservation of seats for women at the local government level, in rural and urban areas. This has been hailed as a watershed achievement in the empowerment of women, and around one million women have come in so far as decision makers at the Panchayat level.[5]

In the present study one of the objectives was to find out the extent of political participation by the respondents. In the villages political participation means mainly participating in the Panchayat activities because with the 73rd amendment 33% seats have been reserved for women and it has become essential for women to take part in village level politics. Some women do so eagerly, others are forced by their men folk who want to reap the benefits in the name of their wives. In the beginning many studies showed that women who were elected to Panchayat posts were mere puppets in the hands of their men, but gradually women have learnt to act on their own and use their power effectively. A study by Devaki Jain proves how successful women Pradhans and Panchayat members have been in developing their villages.

The researcher is already aware that women in Uttaranchal have always been active in social and political movements. Some years back women had spearheaded the political movement for the demand for a new hill state. They had faced all sorts of hardships during the struggle which culminated in the climax which took place on 2nd October 1994 at Rampur Tiraha, in which women were molested, some were raped and some lost their lives. Finally these women were successful in their objective. In the sample villages also the researcher found some women who had participated in the Uttarakhand Movement. and specially one leader who was present at Rampur Tiraha. There were respondents who said they had stood for Panchayat elections and lost, there were some who were ex-members of Panchayat, and some others who are members at present. It was found that while some women took their own decisions and worked independently as Panchayat members, others were controlled by their husbands. Some questions were put to all respondents to find out about their political participation and awareness. The next table divides the respondents into four categories on the basis of their political participation.

**Table 11 : Distribution of Respondents by their Level of Political Participation**

| *S.No.* | *Categories* | *No. of Respondents 'a'* | *No. of Respondents 'b'* | *Percent* |
|---|---|---|---|---|
| 1. | apathetic to politics | 20 | 23 | 21.5 |
| 2. | spectator activity | 46 | 56 | 51 |
| 3. | transitional activity | 22 | 16 | 19 |
| 4. | gladiatorial activity | 12 | 5 | 8.5 |
| | Total | 100 | 100 | 100 |

Table 11 gives a detailed account of the distribution of the respondents into the four categories of political participation, which were described above. Those respondents were considered apathetic who said they had no interest in politics, but actually they may be voting once in a while because Panchayat elections are held in the village itself so they may be forced by others to go and vote. Some of these said they have not voted. The next category had the maximum number of respondents. These women were interested in discussing local politics and also voting both for Panchayat and higher level elections. They were more interested in women candidates for Panchayat and generally voted for them. They mainly discussed the performance of Panchayat members, specially the female members. They realized that the women members had to face difficulties in doing what they want, for the village and the women of their villages, through the Panchayat. They also felt that these women members should have greater freedom to decide and act. The next category included 19% respondents. These women took active part in politics. They attended political meetings, they showed their preference for various national or regional parties and some of them were members of such parties. They took part in rallies and worked towards mobilization. The last category includes the most politically active respondents and constitutes 8.5% of the total sample. These are the women who are presently ward members, Up Pradhan or Pradhan of the Panchayat, or have been in the past. The greatest number of such women were found in Navada, where the Pradhan is a Nepali woman and she has been elected from a general constituency, which means that she has defeated men and women in the election. There are two ex-ward members in Navada [a muslim woman and a scheduled caste woman] and an ex-Pradhan of the Panchayat. The Pradhan and Ex-Up Pradhan of Badripur village Panchayat are women. These are reserved seats. In Hansuwala we met a Muslim woman who had fought the election for Panchayat but lost to a Sikh woman of the village. There are women ward members in other villages. The Pradhan of the Markham Grant Panchayat is also a woman but the respondents said that her husband acts on her behalf. There are a couple of ex-ward members too among the respondents. The duties of the Panchayat members are many and some of these women are aware of their duties and try to fulfill them but there are others who do not know much and their husbands act on their behalf. The Pradhan of Navada is Sarla Thapa and she was considered an efficient office bearer by the respondents. The ex-Up Pradhan of Navada, Anita Thapa was also considered very efficient.

Besides the respondents, the researcher met many other village women to collect more information and at one such visit she met Janki Rawat who had participated in the Uttarakhand movement and had been present at Rampur Tiraha when police attacked and ill-treated peaceful protestors who were proceeding to New Delhi in October 1994. She narrated the travails of the women and boys at that time. She said some women were raped. Some boys went missing and were never found. She said that the Government has promised a job to her and other women who had participated in the movement but as yet the promise has not been fulfilled.

Another question which was put to the respondents was about their perception of the effectiveness of women members of Panchayat. We wanted to know what the women thought about the work efficiency of politically active women. Table 12 shows the data.

**Table 12 : Distribution of Respondents by their Views on Effectiveness of Women Panchayat Members**

| *S.No.* | *Categories* | *No. of Respondents 'a'* | *No. of Respondents 'b'* | *Percent* |
|---|---|---|---|---|
| 1. | are effective | 58 | 42 | 50 |
| 2. | not effective | 42 | 58 | 50 |
| | Total | 100 | 100 | 100 |

These data show that exactly half the respondents feel the women members are effective. Let us note that the number of respondents who said women are effective is much higher in Raipur block villages than the number of respondents in Doiwala villages. This is because the more politically active and efficient women are found in Navada and Badripur, while the Pradhan of Markham Grant was said to be dependent on her husband for all actions. This table supports the conclusion that women members of Panchayat in the sample villages are quite effective, because 50% affirmative replies are quite satisfactory considering the performance of our politicians be they men or women.

The respondents were asked about the various programmes being implemented by their Panchayats. Many of them were not aware of the proper names of the different schemes but when it was explained to them they said they knew about it, for instance they knew about Jawahar Rozgar Yojna, but the name has changed now. They also knew about Indira Awas Yojana, though not by its correct name. Some of them have benefited by these schemes. Old age pension is also given to widows and old men It consists of Rs 700 per 6 months. We met some people who get it but they want the amount to be increased. In some schools we saw that the Mid-day Meal Scheme is also being followed. Here again the poor families want the school to give money instead of meal. Another scheme the respondents told us about was that the government gives monetary aid of Rs 20,000 for the marriage of a daughter to families living below poverty line when they show the wedding card to the Pradhan. Many respondents were complaining that all these schemes are not implemented fast. Secondly people who are rich or known to Panchayat members get all the benefits, while the poor people are neglected. This is a common shortcoming which has been pointed out in all evaluations of rural development schemes. But in the final analysis the researcher would say that the government schemes are being implemented to a large extent and poor people are benefiting too, but since they are very poor they feel more should be done for them. There is no doubt that some irregularities and corruption does exist.

When asked whether they took part in the various programmes which are being run by the Panchayat, only 30% respondents said they did so. By these programmes we meant the training programmes or the health camps or the Self Help Group scheme. The details of these programmes will be dealt with in forthcoming chapters.

When asked how was it considered in their villages, for women to take part in politics, 61.5% respondents said it was considered good. This is a very positive attitude and it is characteristic of the hill society where women have always participated in public life and spearheaded social and political as well as environmental movements. Otherwise in most Indian villages it is not considered good for women to take part in politics. Now that there are seats reserved for women, men allow them to stand for election but do every thing else on their own. Thus men get power in an easier way by allowing their women to win elections to the Panchayat rather than trying to win themselves, which is not easy. But in the sample it was learnt that it is not considered bad for women to take part in politics and quite a few women members act on their own and have the cooperation of their husbands. This shows that people in the sample villages are quite liberal in their thinking. Another question asked was if women are active in politics do they take their own decisions or their husbands do so. We wanted to know the perception of the respondents in this regard. The next table gives the detailed answer of this question.

**Table 13 : Distribution of Respondents by their Perception about Decision Making by Women in Politics**

| *S.No.* | *Categories* | *No. of Respondents 'a'* | *No. of Respondents 'b'* | *Percent* |
|---|---|---|---|---|
| 1. | Husband decides | 22 | 34 | 28 |
| 2. | Decides herself | 78 | 66 | 72 |
| | Total | 100 | 100 | 100 |

We see that very few women feel that husbands take decision, specially among the respondents from Raipur villages. This is because the women Pradhans and members of Panchayat in their villages are quite independent and efficient. This shows that in general the women in the sample villages have freedom to take decisions on their own and many do so. Some questions were asked to find out the level of political awareness or legal literacy of the respondents. Generally in our country even urban and educated women are not fully aware of their rights according to the Constitution. The need for legal literacy is now being recognized as essential for empowerment of women. The efforts at legal literacy of ordinary, less educated women by various government and non-government agencies have had a positive effect and awareness is increasing. The following table shows the level of awareness of respondents.

**Table 14 : Distribution of Respondents by their Level of Awareness of Rights**

| *S.No.* | *Categories* | *No. of Respondents 'a'* | *No. of Respondents 'b'* | *Percent* |
|---|---|---|---|---|
| 1. | aware | 36 | 24 | 30 |
| 2. | not aware | 64 | 76 | 70 |
| | Total | 100 | 100 | 100 |

Data show that only 30% respondents are aware of their rights with a greater number in Raipur villages and lesser in Doiwala villages.

Two more connected questions were about knowledge of privileges and special facilities given to women by the government and whether the respondents will be allowed to avail of them if they wanted to. The following tables show the answers to these questions.

**Table 15 : Distribution of Respondents by their Knowledge of Special Facilities for Women**

| *S.No.* | *Categories* | *No. of Respondents 'a'* | *No. of Respondents 'b'* | *Percent* |
|---|---|---|---|---|
| 1. | have knowledge | 30 | 18 | 24 |
| 2. | Don't have knowledge | 70 | 82 | 76 |
| | Total | 100 | 100 | 100 |

**Table 16 : Distribution of Respondents by their being Allower to Avail of the Benefits**

| *S.No.* | *Categories* | *No. of Respondents 'a'* | *No. of Respondents 'b'* | *Percent* |
|---|---|---|---|---|
| 1. | will be allowed | 71 | 55 | 63 |
| 2. | will not be allowed | 29 | 45 | 37 |
| | Total | 100 | 100 | 100 |

These two tables show that nearly three fourth of the respondents do not know about the various facilities and privileges available to women in our country, but 63% of them feel that once they know and want to avail of them they will not be prevented by their families, instead they will be allowed to take advantage of them, be they regarding education or employment. This shows that the attitude of the families is positive towards women's development and women too are very optimistic. Here again the women of Raipur villages had better knowledge and are more optimistic. This is due to their being more in touch with urban people and many educated people living in Ajabpur and Nawada.

Another question was about their view regarding controlling crime against women. They all agreed that crime against women is on the increase. They were given three options to choose method of control. The answers are in the following table.

**Table 17 : Distribution of Respondents by their View about Controlling Crime Against Women**

| *S.No.* | *Categories* | *No. of Respon-dents 'a'* | *No. of Respon-dents 'b'* | *Percent* |
|---|---|---|---|---|
| 1. | increasing women's awareness | 64 | 71 | 67.5 |
| 2. | taking help of law | 35 | 28 | 31.5 |
| 3. | any other | 1 | 1 | 1 |
| | Total | 100 | 100 | 100 |

Data show most of them feel that if women are well informed crime against them can be controlled, because mostly they become victims due to ignorance. In 'any other' the respondent was vague and couldnot give a proper response.

Finally one last question in the domain of political awareness was about the suggestions that the respondents have to make about measures to be taken to empower women. They were given many options to choose from. Some agreed with only one option and some suggested a number of options. The following table gives the details of their options.

**Table 18 : Distribution of Respondents by the Suggestions they gave for Empowerment of Women**

| *S.No.* | *Categories* | *No. of Respondents 'a'* | *No. of Respondents 'b'* | *Percent* |
|---|---|---|---|---|
| 1. | Education | 51 | 57 | 54 |
| 2. | Political power | 9 | 6 | 7.5 |

| | | | | |
|---|---|---|---|---|
| 3. | Economic independence | 57 | 44 | 50.5 |
| 4. | Increasing awareness | 22 | 29 | 25.5 |
| 5. | Increasing Self-confidence | 17 | 19 | 18 |
| 6. | Giving their rights | 2 | 8 | 5 |

This table shows that the respondents give greatest importance to education and then to economic independence in empowering women. They do not consider political power and giving of rights as important as increasing women's awareness. This shows that they feel women can get empowered when they work for it themselves. Probably they did not properly understand the implication of self confidence, hence few opted for it. May be they feel that even if a woman is confident she is taken seriously only when she is economically independent or well educated and this is quite true in practical life. Unless a poor and illiterate woman proves herself to be empowered, people do not take her seriously. Of course political power can help a lot but probably most women feel that all cannot get political power and that is also true.

Environmental protection and tree plantation are also functions of the Panchayats and the researcher wanted to know what was being done in this regard. Anita Thapa said that when she was Up Pradhan in Nawada Panchayat, she had taken up a tree plantation programme and planted many trees with the help of the village women. She was also a member of BDC in the past and in that capacity she did a lot for the village women like encouraging them to form SHGs to achieve economic self reliance. When the respondents were asked about any environment conservation programme being run now, a great majority of them said they did not know of any such programme, but Sharmila, the Anganwadi worker, said that the Block Pramukh who lives in Nawada, brings saplings every year from the Block office and hands them over to the villagers to plant and nurture. This shows that tree plantation is encouraged in the villages. The Pradhans of Jolly Grant and Hansuwala also said that every year they distribute trees for plantation.

The Panchayat performs many other functions which we will discuss in the following chapters.

The data regarding political participation and political awareness of respondents show that women in the sample villages have a good amount of general and political awareness and they feel that if women are elected to Panchayat posts they will be able to perform efficiently on their own. About half the respondents are quite interested in politics and another 19% are quite active in attending party meetings and other transitional activities.8.5% respondents hold political offices now or have held in the past. Only 21.5% respondents said they are not interested in politics but they also have voted once or twice due to pressure of friends or family. They give great importance to education and awareness as well as legal literacy and want to learn more and benefit by the knowledge. This is a very welcome and positive attitude and authorities should make efforts to educate them in various aspects so that they can empower themselves.

## References

1. Narasimhan S 1999 Empowering Women Sage Publications.
2. Rahman Z 2005 Women and Society Kalpaz Publications.
3. Haralambos 1980 Sociology-Themes and Perspectives OUP.
4. Desai & Krishna Raj Women and Society in India [1987] Ajanta Books.
5. Narasimhan S 1999 Empowering Women Sage Publications.

# 7

# Decision Making Process and Women

Decision making is a mental process, based on conscious reasoning. It is a process by which an evaluation of the meaning and consequence of alternative line of conduct is made.[1] In our society it is generally felt that women are not competent enough to take important decisions, so much so that all their personal decisions also are taken by their men folk. Decisions regarding education, marriage, career, child birth, etc. are purely personal but girls and women are not allowed to take these decisions on their own. Today, due to education and economic independence women have started taking part in decision making process in the family and are also taking independent decisions, but this is confined to a small number, mostly in urban areas. In the villages generally women are not consulted in making important decisions like property or land related decisions, but they do have a say in various other family matters because it is they who are responsible for these matters. They also have a say in some agricultural activities. A study by Singh [1968] shows that women participated in greater number in decision-making with repect to seed storage, winnowing, care of animals and harvesting among some selected farm operations. It was also found that in the above operations husband and wife decided together, while husband decided alone about use of fertilizers and new tools. It has been noted that roles of husbands and wives in decision-making are determined more by their perceived needs of farm and household than by culturally determined patterns. Thus rural women take part in those decisions which are related to their sphere of activity, both at home and in the farm. But very often women have to agree to the decisions of the menfolk even if they have some reervations about them. This is true of all women, be they rural or urban, educated or uneducated.

Political participation also entails decision-making. As we have seen in the previous chapter, today rural women have started participating in the village level politics by becoming members of the Village Panchayat. These women members and Pradhans have proved that they are capable of taking good decisions and implementing them to promote welfare and progress. We have also seen that in many cases the decisions are taken by the husbands. It is difficult to make any generalization because the decision-making power of a woman depends on her potential and her urge or desire to do so. Some women are competent but do not assert themselves. Women have to be motivated to develop their reasoning and potential and then to assert themselves. Decision-making is an important tool of empowerment. A woman who can choose from various alternatives and decide what is best for her is an empowered woman. But to make correct decisions she has to use her intellect. Awarenes and education sharpens the intellect. There are instances of women being effective in decision-making and implementation because they have been motivated and made aware of their rights. Narasimhan gives many examples of illiterate and poor Harijan women from Andhra villages being able to take their own decisions and also to challenge government officials' decisions and demanding accountability after being exposed to motivation and training camps set up by the NGO, AWARE She also writes how these women have now started voting as they wish and not as ordered by their husbands.[2]

In this chapter we will dicuss in detail how far the repondents in the present study, feel and are actually involved, in the decision-making processes in their families and in the village community. Certain questions were put to them to find out their role in various decision-making processes. The following tables present their answers to these questions.

**Table 19 : Distribution of Respondents by their being Consulted by Husbands in Taking Important Decisions**

| *S.No.* | *Categories* | *No. of Respondents 'a'* | *No. of Respondents 'b'* | *Percent* |
|---|---|---|---|---|
| 1. | are consulted | 73 | 73 | 73 |
| 2. | are not consulted | 27 | 27 | 27 |
| | Total | 100 | 100 | 100 |

This table shows that respondents in both groups of villages have anwered in exactly the same way. A little more than two-third repondents say that their husbands consult them in taking important decisions. The researcher feels for rural women this is a positive phenomenon. Considering that nearly half of them are illiterate, it shows that they are still considered capable of taking correct decisions and have an importance for their husbands, since 73% of them are consulted in decision-making.

Next they were asked if they are allowed to take important decisions on their own. We stressed on 'allowed' rather than 'able' because even if they are able they are not allowed to do as they please, very often. This is not only true of rural women but quite often it is true of educated, urban women. Generally women are not allowed to take their own decisions and this has become a tradition so much so that many women feel they are not capable of taking decisions independently. This is a glaring example of 'gender conditioning', where women are brainwashed for generations and finally they become diffident. The next table shows the answer to the question on taking independent decisions.

**Table 20 : Distribution of Respondents by their being Allowed to Take Important Decisions Independently**

| *S.No.* | *Categories* | *No. of Respondents 'a'* | *No. of Respondents 'b'* | *Percent* |
|---|---|---|---|---|
| 1. | are allowed | 36 | 34 | 35 |
| 2. | are not allowed | 64 | 66 | 65 |
| | Total | 100 | 100 | 100 |

This table shows that a little more than one third respondents say they are allowed to take independent decisions. There is not much difference among respondents of the two groups of villages. The researcher feels this also is a positive sign considering they are less educated, tradition bound rural women. The two sets of data show that men believe in giving importance to their wives but would like them to take decisions jointly rather than independently. Secondly, more often than not in joint decisions women agree with their husbands' decision. The answers to the above two questions show that participation of respondents in decision-making process, specially within family, is quite satisfactory. The researcher would like to quote here from National Family Health Surveys' data regarding percentage of married women involved in decision-making about own health care. The data show that in younger age groups women are less involved in decision making, e.g., [38.6% in 15-19 yrs and 45% in 20-24 yrs] while older women are involved more e. g [59.3% in 40-44 yrs and 60.1% in 45-49 yrs] . Data also show that percentage of rural women involved in decision making is 49% and of urban women is 58.9%.[3]

As mentioned earlier women generally have no say in the matter of their marriage and selection of marriage partner; but with changing times, today both boys and girls are consulted by most parents when arranging marriages. May be girls are not consulted to the same extent as boys in traditional homes, whether in rural or urban areas, because of the gender discrimination prevalent in our society. On the other hand, love marriages are becoming quite common and the law also favours the individual in such matters as adult boys and girls can marry into any caste or religion according to law. Many parents forbid such marriages and some times punish the boy and girl very severely, specially in villages. There are cases where boys and girls have been hacked to death for marrying outide their caste. Most often the village elders and the Caste Panchayat ostracise them and they are forced to flee the village. The respondents were asked two questions regarding the marriage of daughters. The first question was whether the mothers are consulted while fixing the marriage and the second was whether they feel girls should be given the freedom to choose life partner. The answers to these questions are shown in the following tables.

**Table 21 : Distribution of Respondents by their Answer to Mother Being Consulted in Fixing Daughter's Marriage**

| S.No. | Categories | No. of Respondents 'a' | No. of Respondents 'b' | Percent |
|---|---|---|---|---|
| 1. | is consulted | 95 | 94 | 94.5 |
| 2. | is not consulted | 5 | 6 | 5.5 |
| | Total | 100 | 100 | 100 |

An overwhelming majority says that mothers are consulted in fixing daughter's marriage. This shows that importance is given to mother's decision making ability hence she is consulted. This is quite natural because a mother is very close to her daughter and can take the most appropriate decision for her marriage. Once again it is a very satisfactory finding.

**Table 22 : Distribution of Respondents by their View Regarding Whether Girls should be Allowed to Marry According to their Wishes**

| *S.No.* | *Categories* | *No. of Respondents 'a'* | *No. of Respondents 'b'* | *Percent* |
|---|---|---|---|---|
| 1. | should be allowed | 67 | 71 | 69 |
| 2. | should not be allowed | 33 | 29 | 31 |
| | Total | 100 | 100 | 100 |

This table shows that the respondents have a very liberal view, which is generally not expected from rural, traditional women. The researcher feels that the main reason for this attitude is that today a daughter's marriage has become a very big problem for parents and it is very difficult for them to find a suitable groom within the caste and also to pay a big dowry, hence women feel that if a girl wants to marry some boy, then the parents should agree as it will solve the problem of selection as well as dowry, in most cases, amicably. This also shows that the respondents are adopting a very practical as well as secular approach by not giving importance to the prevalent customs and traditions. Quite often girls like to marry boys from some other caste or community, thus the respondents appear to condone this modern practice of inter caste marriage. One reason for women taking this liberal view is that today most girls are quite sensible and choose partners who are eligible and would be able to support them. Secondly, if the girls are refused their choice they may rebel and bring a bad name to the family; if they don't rebel then they may remain unmarried because it is very difficult for parents to arrange the marriage. Various factors like education of girls, their employment, their awareness, their feeling of independence, the problem of dowry, the lack of suitable match within the caste are all responsible for parents consenting to love marriages. Still, the answer of the respondents just expresses their view, it does not prove that they will agree to their own daughter marrying a person of her choice and that too of another caste or community. This answer also shows that those respondents who said girls should be allowed to marry according to their wishes are probably doing so because they themselves did not get this chance hence they want the younger generation and their own daughters to get this chance. When asked about education or other facilities too, it is commonly seen that mothers would like their daughters to get all the opportunities that they did not get themselves.

The next questions which were put to the respondents try to find out how they decide about certain issues which concern women. Their answers show their attitudes and their choices and these are directly related to decision making process.

**Table 23 : Distribution of Respondents by their View Regarding Women Working with Men Today**

| *S.No.* | *Categories* | *No. of Respondents 'a'* | *No. of Respondents 'b'* | *Percent* |
|---|---|---|---|---|
| 1. | yes they should | 89 | 83 | 86 |
| 2. | no they should not | 11 | 17 | 14 |
| | Total | 100 | 100 | 100 |

An overwhelming majority says that women should work with men today, the percentage being slightly greater in the villages of Raipur block. This shows that the respondents are quite modern in their outlook and want women to assert their equality by working with men. Most of the repondents are not working outside home but they are highly in favour of it. The answer also shows that they realise the importance of economic independence for a woman. This is a very satisfactory answer from the point of view of women's empowerment and the researcher feels that the respondents show the ability to make a correct decision by favouring women's working with men. The small number of respondents who gave a negative reply appear to be bound by tradition and hence feel it is not correct for women to work with men. The respondents from villages of Raipur block appear to be more modern in their outlook.

The next two questions are about improvement in women's status and the main factors that are responsible for it. The respondents were asked whether they feel that women have a better status now and if so what are the main reasons for it.

**Table 24 : Distribution of Respondents by their View Regarding Status of Women Today**

| *S.No.* | *Categories* | *No. of Respondents 'a'* | *No. of Respondents 'b'* | *Percent* |
|---|---|---|---|---|
| 1. | have a better status | 90 | 86 | 88 |
| 2. | don't have better status | 10 | 14 | 12 |
| | Total | 100 | 100 | 100 |

Again an overwhelming majority says women's status has improved today, which is quite true, both in urban and rural areas, according to various development indices; but a small number says it has not improved. They probably feel that in the patriarchal set up women continue to face oppression and injustice besides facing new problems that have arisen out of modern development like marginalization in economy and bad effects of deforestation etc. Thus their answer too makes sense. The majority view that status of women has improved shows that most women have made a correct judgement of the situation, hence they possess good decision making ability.

When asked about the reasons or factors that have improved women's status today, the respondents gave many answers; most of them gave more than one factor as their answer. The following table shows their answers.

**Table 25 : Distribution of Respondents by the Factors they Consider Responsible for Improvement in Women's Status**

| *S.No.* | *Factors* | *No. of Respondents 'a'* | *No. of Respondents 'b'* | *Percent* |
|---|---|---|---|---|
| 1. | education | 14 | 11 | 12.5 |
| 2. | employment | 29 | 25 | 27 |
| 3. | More independence | 50 | 57 | 53.5 |
| 4. | freedom to go out | 28 | 24 | 26 |
| 5. | late marriage | 4 | 2 | 3 |
| 6. | political power | 20 | 18 | 19 |
| 7. | smaller family | 18 | 15 | 16.5 |

The data show that the respondents feel the biggest factor responsible for better status, is greater independence that women have today. Actually this greater independence is also due to some other factors like change in the social set up, spread of education, spread of modern and liberal ideas, influence of western culture, mass media etc. The next important factors for the respondents are employment and freedom to go outside. These two factors are inter-related and have contributed to women's confidence, thus improving their status. Surprisingly, the respondents do not consider education very important, while they give more importance to factors like smaller family and political power. The researcher feels that in the rural set up there are few highly educated women whereas there are many women who have become self reliant by taking part in politics or by starting their own business after receiving some vocational training, so the respondents feel education is not very important for improving status of rural women. The factor of smaller family is also important from a practical point of view because smaller family generally means a nuclear family and it helps to improve the wife's status. The table shows that both groups of respondents have given more or less similar answers.

Two hypothetical questions were put to the respondents to find out their decision making ability. They were asked that if they get a financial aid from the government for welfare and empowerment of women, what would they do. Their answers were many; the details are given in the table below.

**Table 26 : Distribution of Respondents by What They Would Do to Empower Women if Government Aid is Available**

| *S.No.* | *Alternatives* | *No. of Respondents 'a'* | *No. of Respondents 'b'* | *Percent* |
|---|---|---|---|---|
| 1. | start training centres | 33 | 36 | 34.5 |
| 2. | provide sewing machines etc. | 58 | 43 | 50.5 |
| 3. | start literacy centres | 30 | 18 | 24 |
| 4. | give loans | 6 | 3 | 4.5 |
| 5. | no answer | 9 | 11 | 10 |

About half of the respondents said they would provide women with some asset or means for earning a livelihood. Since most common machine they can use is a sewing machine, it has been mentioned. This shows they feel economic independence is very important for women's empowerment and welfare. About one third said they would open training centres. This again aims at providing employment so this alternative also gives importance to economic self reliance. Very few feel that giving loans can empower women and this is what experts and renowned feminists also feel. Giving loans is not a permanent solution to women's problems, they have to be made self reliant and self confident to become empowered. Thus the respondents show great mental maturity through their choice of options for empowerment of women. There is not much difference in the answers of the two groups except for a greater number of respondents from villages in Raipur block giving importance to literacy. A small per cent of respondents were not able to decide what they would do, probably it was difficult for them to visualise themselves as donors.

The next question was if they became Pradhans of Panchayat what all would they do. There were many answers and most were multiple answers. The details are given below.

**Table 27 : Distribution of Respondents by their Answer to What they Would Do if They Become Pradhans of Panchayat**

| *S.No.* | *Activities* | *No. of Respondents 'a'* | *No. of Respondents 'b'* | *Percent* |
|---|---|---|---|---|
| 1. | adult literacy | 22 | 26 | 24 |
| 2. | employment facilities | 22 | 27 | 24.5 |
| 3. | start self help groups | 7 | 13 | 10 |
| 4. | implement all schemes | 56 | 33 | 44.5 |
| 5. | provide health & hygiene | 2 | 3 | 2.5 |
| 6. | solve problems | 20 | 16 | 18 |
| 7. | promote total development | 18 | 14 | 16 |

This table shows that the respondents are well aware of the potential of a Pradhan and have mentioned all the important activities that are expected of an efficient Pradhan. Thus they show good judgement and mature thinking. Both groups of respondents have shown the same priority, i.e., giving most importance to implementation of schemes, and then to employment and adult literacy, next to problem solving and so on. These priorities also show good reasonng and judgement. The only big difference in the two groups is that more than half the respondents of villages of Raipur block have mentioned implementation of schemes as their choice while in the other group only one third respondents do so. Once again this shows that the former respondents are more aware and more practical in their thinking.

Here the researcher would like to present an account of some women Pradhans in Garhwal hills who have shown very good decision-making ability and helped a lot in the welfare of their villages by efficient functioning. A news item in The Times of India says that Guddi Devi, the gram pradhan of Kinath village and Sobah Jual, gram pradhan of Khutirra village, in Nainidanda Block of Pauri have made a mark by doing exemplary work for their villages, in the form of constructing schools, taking up development work and keeping in touch with Block office to get work done. When their pleas were not listened to they have organised Dharna at the tehsil to achieve their objective. This assertiveness and public decision making has come to them due to the training and inspiration they received from PRAGATI team of the Uttaranchal NGO, RLEK which works for rural people.[4] Narasimhan has also shown how insipiration by an NGO made rural women bold and assertive. The women in the present sample already have a good judgement and if they were to receive some training and encouragement they would also excel, both at family level and community level, in performing welfare activities.

Some questions were asked about dowry, marriage age, divorce and sexual harrament. Most of these will be dealt with in later chapters. Here the researcher would like to discuss their response to the question about sexual harrasment because it is connected with the questions asked earlier in this chapter. When most of the respondents answered that status of women is better today and women should go out to work with men, they were also asked whether crime against women has increased. Almost all agreed it had. So they were asked to choose from various alternatives which would be best to prevent sexual harrassment. The next table shows their answers.

**Table 28 : Distribution of Respondents by their Choice of Alternative to Protect Against Sexual Harrament**

| *S.No.* | *Alternatives* | *No. of Respondents 'a'* | *No. of Respondents 'b'* | *Percent* |
|---|---|---|---|---|
| 1. | training for self defence | 57 | 56 | 56.5 |
| 2. | avoid going out alone | 14 | 24 | 17 |
| 3. | avoid going out at night | 35 | 19 | 27 |
| 4. | do not attract men | 8 | 4 | 6 |

The answers of the two groups are quite similar except that respondents of Raipur villages stress more on avoiding going out at night and of Doiwala on avoiding going out alone. This may be according to their surroundings and conditions. More than half of all repondents feel women should learn some martial art to protect themselves. This is a very modern view. The researcher feels most respondents may not know much about such training but feel it must be good for modern women.

Decision making ability is an important component of empowerment. When women gain the ability to make independent choices about their activities and control over resources and can overcome subordination, then they are truly empowered.[5] In our country women were not allowed to take their own decisions earlier. Now efforts are being made to involve women in decision making process at all levels, by the government and due to many changes, women are also taking greater part in family decisions too. In this chapter we have seen that the respondents in the sample are quite capable of taking correct decisions and they are also given a chance to take part in decision-making. Quite a few of them are able to take decisions independently. This shows that the respondents are in a satisfactory position with regard to their role in decision-making process.

## References

1. Laxmi Devi A Rural Women.
2. Narasimhan S Empowering Women.
3. Bose Ashish Women's Empoerment through Capacity Building.
4. Chopra Jaskiran Times of India, dated May 1st 2006.
5. Dhar S N Micro-Finance for Women.

# 8

# Women's Access to Basic Facilities

Our country is predominantly rural and right since the time of independence conscious efforts are being made to improve the condition of villages, because at the time of independence our villages were in very poor condition. In the first five year plan rural development was given top priority and the Community Development Programme was started for this purpose. Although this programme was not very successful in achieving all it objectives it was instrumental in providing lasting assets and basic infrastructure to villages, thus improving living conditions to some extent. From the 80s IRDP was started all over the country for rural development and many schemes have been implemented since then to provide basic amenities like safe drinking water, shelter, nutrition, health care, sanitation, electrification, transport and communication facilties etc. to villagers. The 8th Plan laid stress on human resource development and gave priority to provision of minimum basic needs to the masses. The 9th Plan too laid stress on this at the same time it adopted women's empowerment as one of its primary objectives. It attempted convergence of existing services, resources, infrastructure and man power available in both women-specific and women-related sectors. The 10th Plan spells out a three pronged strategy for empowering women, in which the first step is social empowerment, aiming at providing easy and equal access to women to all the basic minimum services so as to enable them to realise their full potential.[1] Inspite of all these efforts much remains to be done to provide a satisfactory living standard to the masses in rural areas, specially women.

It is sad that nearly 60 years after independence and after implementation of ten national plans, people in the villages still do not have access to basic facilities like drinking water, health care, proper nutrition, housing etc. in our country. Bhose writes, "there are about 6 lakhs villages with 600 million people living in them. The problem most of them face are innumerable; they are socially oppressed, economically backward and exploited and generally deprived of facilities like health, education, transportation, communication and even denied basic amenities like protected drinking water, food, clothing, shelter etc. As a result they are prone to poverty, illiteracy, ignorance, illhealth and multitudes of exploitations."[2] Rural people are deprived of basic amenities and infrastructure. Sanitation is poor. There is absence of toilets, which is specially very inconvenient for women. Writing about the problems faced by women of rural Garhwal in satisfying basic needs, Sudesh Arya notes that these women have to work hard for long hours in homes and fields but they do not get proper nutrition hence they are weak and underweight. They do not get milk, eggs, vegetables or even dals to eat and subsist mainly on cereals. Due to unhygienic conditions like absence of drainage, waste disposal system and toilets, these women suffer illhealth. Their homes are not properly ventilated. Living in close proximity to animals also leads to disease. Health services are not available. Drinking water has to be brought from far off streams.

Access to facilities is affected by gender-discrimination. Generally women do not have the same access to facilities like health care, nutrition, education etc, as men. In the words of Desai and KrishnaRaj, in the household girls and women get a lesser share in the distribution of health goods and services [including nutrition, medical care and rest] generally but in distribution of labour they get major share of responsibilities. Not only in our country but all over the world less attention is paid to the nutrition, health, immunisation and education of girls than that of the boys. This is the result of cultural conditioning, wherein women are considered less important than men, although they do more work than men. In our villages too women are considered inferior to men, so their access to various amenities is more restricted than that of men. As mentioned above women in the villages of Garhwal do not eat as nutritious food as the men. They work for longer hours and hardly have any rest and relaxation, whereas men folk relax at will. Literacy rates are low in villages but female literacy rates are still lower.

It is true that rural men also suffer from lack of basic amenities and infrastructure, but what needs to be stressed here is that what ever facilities are available in the villages are generally not available to the same extent to both men and women. In this chapter we will find out to what extent the respondents have access to basic facilities and also the extent of gender-discrimination in access to these facilities.

Before presenting the answers of the respondents to the questions put to them it is advisable to discuss the various facilities which were observed in the sample villages by data collectors and were mentioned by the other villagers in informal talks. Regarding education, it was seen that there are government primary schools in all villages. Boys and girls were seen to attend in equal numbers. There are secondary schools in big villages; and some intercolleges also and many private English medium schools. Names of some schools were given in the second chapter. Sarva Shiksha Abhiyan is also running in Nawada and Jolly Grant. Primary health centres are found in some villages, like Nawada, Mothrowala Bhaniawala and Hansuwala. People of Ajabpur and Mothrowala said they go to private doctors in the village.

Villagers in Markham Grant said that the young doctors from Himalayan Institute of Medical Sciences, close by come once in a while to distribute medicines. Immunisation facilities are available at Primary health centres. There are Anganwadis in some villages. At these centres there are trained employees who take care of children in the age group 0–6 yrs and give them nutritious food and immunisation. Nutrition of pregnant and lactating mothers is also taken care of. These women are given knowledge of basic hygiene and health care. Kishori Balika, i.e., girls between 11—18 yrs are also called twice a month to give them some knowledge of hygiene etc. There are schemes for education and nutrition of girl child which are implemented in the villages. There are three Anganwadis in Raipur block villages in the sample and two in the Doiwala block villages. The Anganwadi Sahayika collects the children from their homes and then drops them in the afternoon. Many facilities are provided at the Panchayat Ghar also, for instance there is ANN centre at Mothrowala Panchayat Ghar. At Nawada Panchayat Ghar Vocational training is provided to Scheduled caste boys and girls. Water taps and hand pumps were seen in village homes and also in public places for the poor.

Questions regarding access to basic facilities in the village were put to the respondents at first. Later they were asked whether any distinction was made in providing these amenities and facilities to boys and girls or men and women. The following tables show the details.

**Table 29 : Distribution of Respondents by their View on Satisfaction of Household Needs with Ease**

| *S.No.* | *Categories* | *No. of Respondents 'a'* | *No. of Respondents 'b'* | *Percent* |
|---|---|---|---|---|
| 1. | yes, they are satisfied | 50 | 55 | 52.5 |
| 2. | No, they are not | 50 | 45 | 47.5 |
| | Total | 100 | 100 | 100 |

This table shows that a little more than half the respondents say their needs are satisfied easily which is a good indication. There isn't much difference in the two groups in fact in the first group the number of those who are satisfied is less. This may be either because their needs are more or because the poorer people see the richer ones in better condition so they are not satisfied as their aspirations are higher.

The next questions were about availability of water, both for drinking and for other household purposes. Water is the most essential commodity and its easy availabilty shows the level of development of rural areas. In the sample villages, taps and hand pumps were noticed in many houses but the really poor had to take water from a common pump or tap. Tapwater is not available continuously but comes at fixed times.

**Table 30 : Distribution of Respondents by their View Regarding Availability of Drinking Water**

| *S.No.* | *Categories* | *No. of Respondents 'a'* | *No. of Respondents 'b'* | *Percent* |
|---|---|---|---|---|
| 1. | satisfactory | 36 | 31 | 33.5 |
| 2. | not satisfactory | 45 | 48 | 46.5 |
| 3. | bad | 19 | 21 | 20 |
| | Total | 100 | 100 | 100 |

According to the data, 20 per cent of the respondents feel that the system of provision of drinking water is bad, while another 46.5 per cent feel it is not satisfactory, which shows they feel it is not too bad. Only one third of the respondents are satisfied with the availability of drinking water. The researcher, on the basis of her observation, feels the condition is not so bad. Water was available at taps and hand pumps in most villages and homes. There are a few wells also. Irrigation facilities were reported to be less in some villages, but that was not a main concern of this research. These data have to be interpreted in the light that the respondents felt that if they highlighted their problems they might get some more benefits from the government. Inspite of explaining to them often that the researcher can only report their responses and not provide them any financial aid, they expected that the report would help in getting them more aid. Of course the water supply may be erratic, specially in summer months, which is quite common in cities too. The data were collected in summer. The next question was about the sources of water. They were asked from where did they collect water for household purposes. Their answers are given in the following table.

**Table 31 : Distribution of Respondents by the Sources from which they Collect Water for Household Purposes**

| *S.No.* | *Sources* | *No. of Respondents 'a'* | *No. of Respondents 'b'* | *Percent* |
|---|---|---|---|---|
| 1. | tap | 75 | 83 | 79 |
| 2. | hand pump | 21 | 14 | 17.5 |
| 3. | well | 4 | 3 | 3.5 |
| | Total | 100 | 100 | 100 |

The data show that 79 per cent respondents get water from taps for their needs. It is obvious that they must be getting their drinking water also from the taps. Hence it becomes clear that their dissatisfaction about drinking water is due to erratic supply. A little less than one fifth of the respondents use hand pumps and very few use wells. It appears there are more hand pumps in the villages of Raipur block.

The next questions were about health care, nutrition, adult education, training programes for women, any other special facilities for women and so on. The following tables show the findings.

**Table 32 : Distribution of Respondents by their Response to Question on Presence of Primary Health Centres**

| S.No. | Categories | No. of Respondents 'a' | No. of Respondents 'b' | Percent |
|---|---|---|---|---|
| 1. | yes there are | 55 | 50 | 52.5 |
| 2. | no, there aren't | 45 | 50 | 47.5 |
| | Total | 100 | 100 | 100 |

This table shows that nearly half the respondents said there are no primary health centres. As mentioned above, it was noticed that not all villages had primary health centres. At some centres medical personnel were not available regularly. In Bhaniawala the villagers said that a health worker comes every week. Immunisation is done at regular intervals in almost all villages. Most villagers said that they have to go to town for any big health problem, for instance, in villages close to Dehradun, people go to Doon Hospital and in villages close to Doiwala people go to the hospital in Doiwala or to the Himalayan Institute which is in Jolly Grant. As mentioned above there are many private clinics in bigger villages. There are primary health centres in some villages and in others the Aanganwadi also takes care of health and nutrition of children and pregnant as well as lactating mothers. In Mothrowala the Primary health centre is open ever day and it was established in 1955. At the centre medical check up is done for small children and pregnant ladies regularly. The health workers also go on field work to check children and women and distribute medicines if required. In every health centre there is a female health worker per 1000 people and she takes care of immunisation of children. She also accompanies pregnant women to hospital if there is need during labour and stays till the delivery. Generally women prefer to deliver at home in the presence of a nurse or trained mid wife. Family planning devices like Nirodh and Mala D or copper T are also provided at Primary Health Centres. Medicines for common ailments are provided to all. There is a plan to hold health camps ever month. Supplementary nutrition and vitamins are provided to pregnant women, young girls and to children below 6 years of age. The response of the respondents also shows that they are not aware of some facilities while many think that going to private doctors or big hospitals is better, therefore they do not know much about the health centres in their villages. When asked how many went regularly to the health centres, only one third said they do so. This again shows their lack of interest in village health centre.

**Table 33 : Distribution of Respondents by their Response to Question About Nutrition in Villages**

| *S.No.* | *Categories* | *No. of Respondents 'a'* | *No. of Respondents 'b'* | *Percent* |
|---|---|---|---|---|
| 1. | nutrition is good | 66 | 72 | 69 |
| 2. | nutrition not good | 34 | 28 | 31 |
| | Total | 100 | 100 | 100 |

More than two third of the respondents are satisfied with the nutrition available to the family members and this is a positive sign.

With regard to nutrition, the respondents were also asked how many of them were vegetarian and how many were non-vegetarian. In the Doiwala villages half the respondents were vegetarians while in the Raipur villages only one third were vegetarian. This may be because of greater number of Nepalis and Muslims in these villages. Many Garhwalis also are non-vegetarian. The respondents were also asked about the food grains, vegetables and fruits grown in their fields and villages. They named rice, wheat and maize among food grains, mango, leechi and guava among fruits and quite a few vegetables like lady's finger, peas, beans, ridge gourd, bitter gourd, pumpkin and cucumber. In villages milk is also easily available. Separate questions were asked about milk.

**Table 34 : Distribution of Respondents by their Ownerhip of Milch Cattle**

| S.No. | Categories | No. of Respondents 'a' | No. of Respondents 'b' | Percent |
|---|---|---|---|---|
| 1. | have cattle | 25 | 62 | 43.5 |
| 2. | do not have cattle | 75 | 38 | 56.5 |
| | Total | 100 | 100 | 100 |

This table shows that there is a great difference between the two groups of respondents in this respect. Only one-fourth respondents in Raipur villages have cattle whereas 62% respondents in Doiwala villages own cattle. The main reason for this is that the Pal community, which is a milkman caste, inhabits the Doiwala villages in great numbers. When asked whether milk was sold or used at home, 77% respondents said it was used at home only. This implies that they own either one or two buffalos and therefore do not sell milk. This also implies that the family members, specially children get milk, every day. In Majri Grant there were some rich Pal families who own many cattle and sell milk in huge quantities.

Although there are enough schools for children in the sample villages there aren't enough adult literacy centers. Even if there are centers being run by Panchayats, they are not functioning properly or regularly, as reported by villagers. Sarva Shiksha Abhiyan is also in progress in some villages like Nawada and Jolly Grant, but attendance of adults is poor. Among the respondents only 10% said they know of adult literacy centers and go there to learn to read and write.

This shows that almost all those respondents who are educated have had their education as children and very few have learnt to read and write as adults. Thus there is need to motivate illiterate adults and activate the existent adult literacy centers, to function more efficiently. There is also need to open more literacy centers in all villages to achieve total literacy as soon as possible.

Similarly only 10% respondents said there are special training programmes being run for women in the Panchayats and only 5% said that they are benefiting by them. The fact is that there are special programmes for women being run by Panchayats and NGOs but most of them charge at least a nominal fees for imparting training. In the Nawada Panchayat a special ITI tailoring and cutting course for Scheduled caste boys and girls is being run and charges a nominal fees. When the researcher visited the Panchayat hall two girls were learning drafting from a teacher who had come from Dehradun. This training is provided by the Department of Social Welfare Directorate, Government of Uttaranchal. There are many NGOs providing various types of training but they generally charge about hundred rupees per month which the poor women and girls are not able to pay. The NGO Samarpit provides training free of cost and many girls and women were seen to attend stitching classes there. In Hansuwala a politician has et up a center to teach stitching and embroidery to girls but it also charges a fees of hundren rupees for its courses. Two girls were seen attending a cutting class there. Details of NGO activities will be discussed in a later chapter.

Self Help Groups will be discussed in greater detail in the next chapter but here it is relevant to mention that only 12 respondents in Raipur village and 7 in Doiwala villages said there are self help groups in their village. This is one area where more awareness and encouragement is required, because self help groups are proving effective in improving the economic condition of rural women.

The next two questions are about the type of burner and type of fuel used for cooking. The answers are shown in the following tables.

**Table 35 : Distribution of Respondents by the Type of Burner/Stove they Use for Cooking**

| *S.No.* | *Categories* | *No. of Respondents 'a'* | *No. of Respondents 'b'* | *Percent* |
|---|---|---|---|---|
| 1. | mud chulha | 24 | 39 | 31.5 |
| 2. | keroene stove | 8 | 2 | 5 |
| 3. | gas stove | 68 | 59 | 63.5 |
| | Total | 100 | 100 | 100 |

Data show that nearly two thirds of the respondents use gas stoves, with greater number in Raipur villages than in Doiwala villages. This shows that modern facilities with regard to burners and fuel are available in all villages. On the other hand nearly one thirds of the respondents use mud chulhas which are the traditional burners in villages, with greater numbers using it in Doiwala villages than in Raipur village. It has been noted many times that Raipur villages are comparatively more modern due to proximity to Dehradun. Very few use kerosene stoves. The next table shows use of different fuels.

**Table 36 : Distribution of the Respondents by the Type of Fuel they Use for Cooking**

| *S.No.* | *Categories* | *No. of Respondents 'a'* | *No. of Respondents 'b'* | *Percent* |
|---|---|---|---|---|
| 1. | wood | 59 | 67 | 63 |
| 2. | cow dung cakes | 35 | 44 | 39.5 |
| 3. | kerosene | 9 | 7 | 8 |
| 4. | charcoal | 4 | 5 | 4.5 |
| 5. | gas | 68 | 59 | 63.5 |

Data show that the respondents use combinations of fuels for cooking and other burning purposes, for instance they use wood together with cow dung and gas. Cow dung and wood is available free of cost so all poor villagers use these fuels but even those who possess gas or kerosene stoves, may use cow dung or wood sometimes. Some use charcoal occasionally for heating water. Cooking gas is used very carefully as it is quite expensive, so it is supplemented with other fuels. This is done quite often in cities too. It is not only the cost but the difficulty in availability of gas cylinders that forces people to use gas sparingly. The table shows that while 63.5% use gas, 63% use wood, thus it is an equal mix of modern and traditional fuel use. Nearly 40% use cow dung cakes as it is easily available.

After finding out about access to various basic facilities, the respondents were next questioned about the presence or absence of gender bias in access to these facilities. As mentioned above there is a common tendency in all societies of not providing equal access to both sexes to various facilities. Women are generally denied access, or have very limited access, to many facilities as compared to men. The worst part is that the women are so conditioned that they feel this discrimination is correct and help to perpetrate it. Girls are taught to forgo many facilities that are available to boys, by their mothers. Therefore, the respondents were asked whether the boys and girls in their villages and families were treated more or less similarly with regard to health care, nutrition and education. A lesser bias would show that the respondents are quite liberated in their thinking and are moving in the right direction to bring about gender equality in the younger generation. The following tables show their answers.

**Table 37 : Distribution of Respondents by their View Regarding Discrimination in Nutrition of Boys and Girls**

| *S.No.* | *Categories* | *No. of Respondents 'a'* | *No. of Respondents 'b'* | *Percent* |
|---|---|---|---|---|
| 1. | there is discrimination | 9 | 6 | 7.5 |
| 2. | there isn't discrimination | 91 | 94 | 92.5 |
| | Total | 100 | 100 | 100 |

This table shows that there is very little discrimination in nutrition of boys and girls and it is a very positive sign. Related to this there was another question asking the respondents whether women got good nutrition in their villages. In answer 63% respondents said women got good nutrition, while 37% said they did not. The reasons may be both poverty and some discrimination. This shows that there was slightly more gender discrimination among the older generation, which has reduced considerably in the younger generation. This again is a very good sign and shows there is positive social change taking place in this rural society and gender discrimination is decreasing. The next table is about health care and gender discrimination.

**Table 38 : Distribution of Respondents by their View Regarding Discrimination Health Care of Boys and Girls**

| *S.No.* | *Categories* | *No. of Respondents 'a'* | *No. of Respondents 'b'* | *Percent* |
|---|---|---|---|---|
| 1. | there is discrimination | 1 | 6 | 3.5 |
| 2. | there isn't discrimination | 99 | 94 | 96.5 |
| | Total | 100 | 100 | 100 |

This table also shows there is hardly any discrimination in providing health care to boys and girls in the sample villages which is a very progressive phenomenon. All over the country it is being noticed that health of women and girl child is neglected. Hence it is really commendable that there is very little discrimination in these villages. A couple of respondents in Majri Grant had said that equal importance is not given to immunization of girls. This should be rectified. Immunization is any way free of cost so there should be no discrimination at all. Here again women were also questioned about whether in their view women received proper health care in their villages. In answer 62% respondents said women get good health care while 38% said they do not. These numbers are similar to those regarding nutrition and we see that there is greater discrimination in older generation. Besides poverty and gender bias, women's attitude towards their own health is also responsible for their being neglected. Women generally feel they should not give importance to their health needs or other needs, but young girls today demand all that the boys get and parents also feel they should get equal share in goods and services available to family. Mothers feel their daughters should not suffer what they themselves had suffered. Due to all these factors now there is less discrimination.

Next they were questioned about discrimination in education of boys and grls. The following table shows the details.

**Table 39 : Distribution of Respondents by their View Regarding Discrimination in Education of Boys and Girls**

| *S.No.* | *Categories* | *No. of Respondents 'a'* | *No. of Respondents 'b'* | *Percent* |
|---|---|---|---|---|
| 1. | there is dicrimination | 14 | 15 | 14.5 |
| 2. | there isn't dicrimination | 86 | 85 | 86.5 |
| | Total | 100 | 100 | 100 |

This table shows that there is some discrimination in education of boys and girls and this is very natural because boys have to earn a living at all costs while girls have an option. Therefore parents who are not very rich naturally give greater importance to educating boys in such a way that they are able to find employment soon after studies where as school education is considered good enough for girls, or may be some college education too if it is easily available. Girls are also allowed to do BA and MA privately. This is true not only about Indian society but all over the world. Considering that the discrimination reported is not much and nearly 90% respondents said that all their children [boys and girls] are being educated, the scenario is quite satisfactory. In today's set up it is equally essential to educate girls and prepare them to find employment, just like boys, but in poor and rural homes it is not possible always to provide strict equality. Some times it is not possible even in middle class homes in cities as professional education is becoming very expensive. So it is reasonable to conclude that there is not much discrimination in education of boys and girls in the sample villages.

In this chapter we have seen that the respondents' access to basic facilities like water, household items, fuel, food, nutrition, health care, education, vocational training for economic independence etc. is of varying degrees. Some facilities are available to a satisfactory extent while many others are not available to a satisfactory extent. For instance adult literacy programmes, training programmes for women and primary health centers in villages are not found in sufficient numbers. There is need to increase the number of these facilities and run them more efficiently. As noted in the Annual report of an NGO working in the area, the non availability of required medicines and inadequate health care in primary health centers are common complaints against the primary health care system in the village community. The health status of poor rural people, specially women and children is not satisfactory. There is also lack of total sanitation in villages. Disposal of waste is not being done in a hygienic way. There is also a lack of toilets in the villages.[3] Transport and communication facilities, though they are improving, are not fully satisfactory. Recently roads are being constructed in bigger villages and bus service has started. Three wheelers are also plying through the main roads of bigger villages, specially in Ajabpur and Nawada. All the above mentioned shortcomings have to be addressed with greater focus. Besides there is also need to motivate the women to make use of the available facilities, because it was noted that women were not keen to go for adult literacy classes. The functioning of all these centers should also improve so that village women are attracted by them. Access to facilities like nutrition, household items, drinking water, fuel etc. was found to be reasonably satisfactory. Most women appeared to be satisfied with the status they have in their families. A positive finding was that hardly any gender discrimination is found in providing facilities to children. Of course among the older generation there is some gender discrimination but that is natural in any patriarchal society. No where was extreme gender discrimination noticed or reported in access to basic facilities.

## References

1. Platform for Action and Working Group on Empowerment of Women-Tenth Plan, Ministry of HRD. Government of India.
2. Bhose Rural Development and NGOs.
3. Samarpit Sewa Sansthan Annual Report 2005-06.

# 9

# Economic Independence of Women

One of the major components of empowerment is economic independence. It is felt that since most women in our society are economically dependent on their men folk they do not have a say in decision making and cannot do any thing on their own. Gradually they lose their power of decision making and their potential to take any initiative and just obey orders This suits the patriarchal system very well, hence the status quo is maintained by socializing girls to be submissive and extremely obedient. It is good to be obedient and also to submit to authority but not to the extent that it hampers one's personality development. Women should be able to act according to their wishes and take their own decisions (of course in consultation with family members). It has been noticed that when women are able to earn a stable income their status improves in the family and they are consulted in family decisions. Earning money by her own efforts also increases a woman's self esteem and self-confidence. In modern times Indian women have started working outside homes in various professions and society has accepted this to a great extent. Even in villages women are working in many new occupations besides working in fields and cottage industries, which they have always done. Today rural women are working as teachers, nurses, beauticians, clerks in offices, sales girls, tailors and technicians. They are also working in various capacities in the PRIs, Aangan wadis, Bal wadis, NGOs etc. Of course just earning money by working outside home does not empower a woman, she should also be able to control her income. Many Indian women earn money over which they have no control. This applies not only to uneducated rural women but also to educated urban women. This is not only due to the patriarchal set up but also due to lack of confidence and guts in the women themselves. They have to learn to fight for their rights. In the words of S N Dhar, Empowerment does not only include increase in women's levels of income, but control over income and assets and participation in community and household decisions. A woman is truly empowered if she can enhance her self confidence and status within her family as independent producer of wealth and provider of finance to her household.'[1] Thus economic independence in the real sense leads to empowerment. Sometimes women have economic independence even if they are not earning themselves when their husbands allow them to spend according to their own decisions. This happens in many households where housewives have a control over expenditure.

It is generally felt that if women are able to earn they will have a better status, hence the Government has always implemented schemes for providing vocational training to women so that they may find employment or start their own business. In this connection loans are also offered to them and there have been schemes to encourage them to save money in their own accounts. Some programmes of this nature are DWCRA, IMY, MSY etc. In 1987 STEP, Support to Training and Employment Programmes, was launched. It aimed to upgrade the skills of the poor and assetless women and provide employment to women in the traditional sectors such as agriculture, dairying, fisheries, handlooms and handicrafts. In addition to training and employment support,

STEP's three special features are 'gender sensitisation', 'women in development inputs' and 'support services'. Since its inception the programme has provided employment to around 1.52 lakh women. The SEP, Socio Economic Programme is implemented by CSWB and gives training to needy women like widows, deserted wives, backward and handicapped women. It takes care of both illiterate and semi literate women. Trades promoted include traditional agro based industries as well as non traditional trades.[2]

Micro finance for women is a comparatively new concept for increasing women's economic independence and thus empowering them. It is being used to help rural women in India. The term micro finance generated awareness mainly in mid 90s after the World Summit for Social Development was held in Copenhagen in 1995. This Summit underscored the significance of access to credit to low income women and vulnerable groups. The World Micro Credit Summit of Washington, in 1997, announced a count down for eradicating poverty of 100 million poorest families, specially women, with micro credit for self employment, by the year 2005. But the real pioneer of micro credit is Prof. Yunus of Bangladesh who set up the Grameen Bank in 1976 with a small capital to give loans to poor rural women.[3] The great success he achieved in empowering rural women has earned him the Nobel Peace Prize for the year 2006. The secretary general of Amnesty International, Irene Khan noted that the Grameen Bank gave loans to the poor, 95% of them being women, and thus, has given them human dignity and economic security. Prof. Yunus has thus contributed to peace by giving economic independence and self confidence to poor rural women, who now have a better status in their families and a better standard of life. In India, as in many other countries, ensuring women's access to credit through micro-credit schemes is a major component of strategies for both poverty alleviation and women's empowerment. Thousands of women's self-help groups have been set up across the country by NGOs and through government programmes like, Rashtriya Mahila Kosh, Indira Mahila Yojna and SGSY. Micro credit through women's SHGs is also a central element of the development vision outlined in the Tenth Five Year Plan.[4]

In the villages of the present study many of the above schemes are in operation. In the village panchayats women and girls are given vocational training which includes stitching, beautician training for girls etc. The researcher saw a stitching class being held in Navada Panchayat for Scheduled caste girls. It is meant also for boys. This training is being offered by the Social Welfare Directorate. It is a one year course which is recognized by the ITI. Besides this, thePanchayat also runs SGRY, SGSY, Indira Awas Yojna etc. At the Aangan wadi centers the Kishori Shakti Yojna is also implemented which aims at increasing awareness and skills of girls in age group 11 to 18 years. Old age pension is given to deserving people and it comprises of Rs 700 per 6 months. There is also a scheme for a grant of Rs 20,000 for the marriage of the daughter in a BPL family. For this the parents have to fix the marriage and then apply for the grant with the Wedding card as proof. The concept of Self-help groups has yet to become popular in these villages but there are some SHGs functioning in Navada, Ajabpur and Mothrowala. A couple of them have been quite successful, like the one named Prerna which is run by Rukmini Joshi and ten other women members, in Mothrowala. This group got a loan of Rs 25,000 from the Government and started a business in pulses. They sell packets of pulses as well as some products made from pulses. They also give loans to village women on small interest. The group has an account in its name in a Mini Bank in Jogiwala, with a deposit of Rs 16,000. Some SHGs are just functioning as lending agencies on small interest rate, while others are producing various items like pickles, dairy products and selling them.

The sample of the present study included 36% respondents who said that they have personal income. Besides these respondents many others said that they were able to spend money according to their wishes within reasonable limits. The objective was to find out how much economic independence is available to these women and what steps are they taking to enhance their economic independence. With this objective various questions were put to them. The following tables show their responses to some questions. First of all they were asked whether it was considered acceptable for women to go out and work in order to earn money. Rural women have always gone out to work in their fields or to collect fodder and fuel, but here the researcher wanted to know whether their working in offices, schools or shops in various capacities was acceptable. The responses are presented in the following table

**Table 40 : Distribution of Respondents by their Response to Whether Working of Women is Acceptable**

| *S.No.* | *Responses* | *No. of Respondents 'a'* | *No. of Respondents 'b'* | *Percent* |
|---|---|---|---|---|
| 1. | it is acceptable | 63 | 68 | 65.5 |
| 2. | it is not acceptable | 37 | 32 | 34.5 |
| | Total | 100 | 100 | 100 |

Data show that nearly two third of the respondents feel that in their village working of women outside home to earn money is acceptable. Next they were asked if they knew some women who worked out side homes in their villages and earned money. They all replied in the affirmative. Next they were asked whether their earning money has improved the prestige of those women. Surprisingly only 55 per cent respondents replied in the affirmative saying that economic independence has improved the status of those women in their families and their prestige has also increased in the village society and other women look up to them. But the rest who replied in the negative said that in some families the men folk do not like the women becoming economically independent while in some a lot of responsibilities are given to them because they are earning thus 45 per cent respondents feel earning money has not affected their prestige. Next they were questioned about how many of them earn a personal income. The responses are in table 41.

**Table 41 : Distribution of Respondents by their Having Personal Income**

| S.No. | Categories | No. of Respondents 'a' | No. of Respondents 'b' | Percent |
|---|---|---|---|---|
| 1. | have personal income | 28 | 44 | 36 |
| 2. | don't have per. Income | 72 | 56 | 64 |
| | Total | 100 | 100 | 100 |

As mentioned above 36% respondents have personal income, in which the number is greater in Doiwala villages than in Raipur Block villages. This may be because men in Raipur villages are better employed hence less women feel the need to earn. The next table shows how much these women earn per month.

**Table 42 : Distribution of Respondents by the Amount of their Monthly Income**

| S.No. | Categories | No. of Respondents 'a' | No. of Respondents 'b' | Percent |
|---|---|---|---|---|
| 1. | less than Rs.500 | 10 | 16 | 13 |
| 2. | Rs 501-1000 | 10 | 8 | 9 |
| 3. | Rs 1001-1500 | 5 | 15 | 10 |

| | | | | |
|---|---|---|---|---|
| 4. | more than Rs 1500 | 3 | 5 | 4 |
| 5. | not applicable | 72 | 56 | 64 |
| | Total | 100 | 100 | 100 |

This table shows that the greatest number of women earn less than Rs 500 per month which is quite low. They might be working as labourers or domestic servants. Very few women earn more than Rs 1500 per month. But more important than the amount they earn is the confidence and dignity they achieve because they are earning by their own efforts. Generally women's work remains unpaid whether it is at home, or in the fields or in the family cottage industry, therefore getting cash in return for their labour invigorates these women and gives them satisfaction and self confidence.

The next question was about how they spend their personal incomes. Table 43 shows the details.

**Table 43 : Distribution of Respondents by the Way they Spend their Personal Income**

| *S.No.* | *Categories* | *No. of Respondents 'a'* | *No. of Respondents 'b'* | *Percent* |
|---|---|---|---|---|
| 1. | For own needs | 0 | 1 | 0.5 |
| 2. | for children | 27 | 31 | 29 |
| 3. | for family members | 1 | 12 | 6.5 |
| 4. | Not applicable | 72 | 56 | 64 |
| | Total | 100 | 100 | 100 |

Data show that an overwhelming majority of earning women says they spend their personal income for their children. This is a most natural attitude of mothers, be they rich or poor; urban or rural. Another point to be noted is that only one respondent said she uses the money for herself. This shows the selflessness of these women, which is now becoming rare among educated, urban women. A sacrificing nature is attributed traditionally to women, but today women are learning that it is not wrong to take care of one's self and spend for one's own needs, specially if one is earning herself. Gradually, as poverty is reduced, rural women too would start spending for their own need satisfaction.

Another question about economic independence that was put to the respondents was whether women in their villages could spend money by themselves, according to their wishes. Of course it was explained that the expenditure should be reasonable and sensible. The answers are shown in the next table.

**Table 44 : Distribution of Respondents by Whether they Can Spend Money According to their Wishes, Themselves**

| *S.No.* | *Categories* | *No. of Respondents 'a'* | *No. of Respondents 'b'* | *Percent* |
|---|---|---|---|---|
| 1. | can spend | 69 | 69 | 69 |
| 2. | cannot spend | 31 | 31 | 31 |
| | Total | 100 | 100 | 100 |

It is seen that the respondents of both groups have replied exactly in the same way and more than two thirds of the respondents feel they can spend money according to their wishes. This shows indirectly that women in the sample enjoy a satisfactory status in their families because most of them are quite satisfied with their economic independence, whether they are earning themselves or not. In this connection the other question was whether they are consulted by their husbands in money matters The responses to this question are presented in the next table.

**Table 45 : Distribution of Respondents by their Being Consulted in Money Matters**

| *S.No.* | *Categories* | *No. of Respondents 'a'* | *No. of Respondents 'b'* | *Percent* |
|---|---|---|---|---|
| 1. | are consulted | 78 | 73 | 75.5 |
| 2. | are not consulted | 22 | 27 | 24.5 |
| | Total | 100 | 100 | 100 |

Once again the answers of the two groups are quite similar with the first group having five more women answering in the affirmative. On the whole more than three fourths of the respondents say they are consulted in money matters. This also shows that the women have a satisfactory status in the family and are given importance in taking decisions about spending money for the family. When women are consulted in taking decisions they are able to express their views and convince other family members about their views. Thus they have a chance of getting things done their way. This increases their self esteem and self confidence. They feel that importance is being given to them and when their views are accepted they feel empowered. In a way it shows they also have some control over financial resources.

Some other questions related to family income were whether the respondents have milch cattle at home and whether the milk is sold. The responses are given below.

**Table 46 : Distribution of Respondents by their Owning Milch Cattle**

| *S.No.* | *Responses* | *No. of Respondents 'a'* | *No. of Respondents 'b'* | *Percent* |
|---|---|---|---|---|
| 1. | have cattle | 25 | 62 | 43.5 |
| 2. | do not have cattle | 75 | 38 | 56.5 |
| | Total | 100 | 100 | 100 |

The table shows that only one fourth respondents in Raipur villages said they have cattle while more than 60 per cent in Doiwala villages have cattle. The Pal community which is found in great numbers in Doiwala villages, specially in Majri Grant and Jolly Grant have dairy farming as their main occupation, where as in Raipur villages few have dairy farming as their main occupation. Out of the 25 who have cattle in group 'a', 17 said milk is sold and money used in family and out of 62 who have cattle in group 'b', 49 said milk is sold for money The rest said that the milk is used by family members as supply is not much. On being asked about growing vegetables at home 35 per cent respondents said they do so. These vegetables are used for family consumption.

Another area where questions were asked was about their dwelling place. In both groups 77 per cent respondents said they have 'pucca' houses and 23 per cent said they live in huts. In the Raipur block villages, 95 per cent respondents owned their houses and only 5 per cent lived in rented houses, while in Doiwala block villages 87 per cent lived in their own houses and 13 per cent in rented houses. These data show that with regard to housing the respondents are in a satisfactory position.

As mentioned earlier, Self Help Groups are not found in great number in sample villages. When asked about membership to self help groups only 12 respondents in Raipur block villages and 7 in Doiwala block villages replied in the affirmative. Thus 9.5% respondents are members of SHGs. Some respondents are running Self Help Groups successfully, though; for instance Rukmini Joshi in Mothrowala, who was mentioned earlier and Savita Devi in Badripur, who is the President of the group. She informed that they got a loan of Rs 23,000 from the Block office. They started a dairy. They also gave loans to members to the tune of Rs 10,000. When one cow in the dairy died the Government paid them insurance money. They are planning to get a bigger loan from the Government this year. On the other hand some respondents said they had started SHGs but now they are not functioning because there was a problem of returning the loans. This was reported in Ajabpur and Nawada. Sharmila and Lalita Sethi in Nawada said their groups are now closed. Earlier Sharmila had 10 members in her group and they sold home made pickles as well as lent money at 2% interest. But the venture was not very successful. Some women said there was a lack of trust among members. If these women are made aware of the benefits of working together and operating through self help groups in an organized way and if they are encouraged by the Panchayat members, there is scope for improvement.

Today, NGOs play a very constructive role in rural development and also in women's empowerment and various studies have shown that they achieve better results than government agencies because they are in closer contact with local people and develop better rapport with them.5 In the present sample villages there are some NGOs working for rural development and women's empowerment. The researcher met with the officials of these NGOs to find out what work they do and what have been their achievements. Samarpit Sewa Sansthan is an NGO in Ajabpur which was set up on 9th December 1992 by Kamla Jaiswal. She is a dedicated social worker and her work has been recognized by the Uttaranchal Government. The Honourable Governor, Shri Sudarshan Agrawal has donated sewing machines to the NGO. It is registered under FCRA Act 1976 and also under Ministry of Finance Government of India. It's a proactive peoples' organization that works towards establishing a progressive, peaceful, secular and just society based on the tenets of equality, fraternity and mutual support. Its mission is to enable people to conquer poverty and inequality, specially in relation to natural resources. It aims to give voice to the voiceless by empowering them through capacity building process and self help concept. Its objectives include the following : to help rural community to develop capabilities and participate in development process; to promote sustainable development of natural resources in Himalayan region; to empower rural women; to revitalize indigenous knowledge and also disseminate newer technologies to increase productivity. Its activities include Natural Resource Management, Water harvesting, Soil and Water Conservation, Testing quality of soil and water by chemical analysis at their Laboratory, training for women in tailoring and handicrafts, promoting self help groups and gender equity in local self governance by training women in Panchayat functioning, creating health awareness and organizing health camps as well as blood donation camps. It also promotes entrepreneur-ship among rural women by helping them set up their business. This NGO is running various programmes like CAPART's Watershed Development Programme, Craft Project and SGSY, Under the Craft Project women are offered one year Diploma course in tailoring, free of cost. The trainees appear for an exam recognized by ITI and get a Certificate on passing the exam successfully. The achievements of Samarpit are many. The NGO has introduced roof top water harvesting in rural areas and in Sahaspur it has built a collection pond with a capacity of 16 lakh tonnes. This has helped the farmers to grow two and even three crops per year. It has helped many of its students to set up their tailoring business and many of them are now successful business women, with a better life style and better status in family and community. Other activities which are successfully carried out include tree plantation, Sampoorna Swachhata Abhiyan for construction of toilets and general cleanliness, awareness generation and motivation among rural women to make them self-reliant. The NGO has provided gainful employment to 69 women so far and has set up 27 SHGs all over the district to empower women in villages.

Koshish is another NGO which is functioning in Doiwala block, close to Hansuwala, Bhaniyawala and other smaller villages. It is mainly interested in providing education and vocational skill to girls. This NGO was started in 2004 by Vipin Handa and his associates who have a men's boutique in New Delhi. Their idea was to train girls and women in tailoring and embroidery and provide raw material to them from Delhi for garment making. The finished goods are then marketed in New Delhi by them. The students are charged a fees of 100 rupees per month. They are offered a one year course in Fashion Designing. They are also taught English, basic computer knowledge and Home Science. Once a month a Doctor visits the institution for free health checkup. Frequently visiting Faculty members are invited for giving Guest Lectures. At present there are about 200 students and the Principal is Mrs. Abha Chandna.

In Hansuwala there is a center for giving vocational training to girls. It is known as Uttaranchal Shikshan Prashikshan Anusandhan Kendra. It was started by the political party, NCP in 2005. The teacher is Kiran and she provided the information that there are two courses being offered to girls and the fees is Rs 100 per month. There is a 6 month course in tailoring and a three month course in painting and embroidery. Presently only six girls have joined the six month course.

In Ajabpur there is a cell of Uttarakhand Mahila Manch. This is a voluntary organization which fights for women's rights in the whole State. It is not registered as an NGO, but it offers legal assistance and counseling to women in need. It also helps in finding employment for women. Kamla Pant and Nirmala Bisht are its representatives and they are well known social workers. A new NGO named Sandhya Deep has been started in Badripur which is working for rural people specially women.

While talking to respondents and their daughters informally, it was found that most women and girls would like to get some vocational training so that they can earn some money but they cannot afford a monthly fees for it. They said that if such training is given free of cost by the Panchayat, it would benefit the poorest of the poor. Today girls would like to train as beauticians and work in beauty parlours. Although one Panchayat offers this training, many others do not. There are three beauty parlours in Nawada, in which girls trained in Dehradun are working. It would be beneficial to poor girls to be offered this training free of cost in their respective villages. Some educated girls are working as teachers in schools and as Aangan wadi workers, some girls are also working in hospitals and clinics as nurses and receptionists. Older women were seen running small shops and tea stalls. In Nawada Draupadi has a big general store. Poor women also work as domestic help in bigger houses.

In conclusion, it can be said that while 36 per cent respondents said they have a personal income, many others are quite satisfied with their economic status in the family since a majority of them feel they can spend according to their wishes and are consulted in financial decisions of the family. Many respondents said that if better vocational training facilities are available in their villages, more women would be able to earn, but many others said they do not have time to go out to work. Their household work keeps them busy. Both these views have weight. Those women who have time would like to work but even those who are busy with household work are doing productive work and if it is recognized as such in their families, they should be satisfied. Therefore they are not very keen to work outside home. The data show in general that the respondents feel they are not at a disadvantage with regard to economic capacity, but it in no way means that they do not have economic problems or that all are economically well off. There are many problems and many respondents are poor, while some are very poor but most of them are satisfied with their position in the prevailing conditions. It is hoped that they get out of this complaisance and try to be more economically sound.

## References

1. Dhar, S.N. 2004, Micro Finance for Women, Northern Book Centre.
2. Verma & Nath, 2005, Women and Rural Development Programmes.
3. Dhar, S.N. 2004, Micro Finance for Women, Northern Book Centre.
4. Burra, Ranadive, Murthy [ed.] 2005, Micro Credit Poverty and Empowerment, Sage Publications.
5. Bhose, 2003, NGOs and Rural Development, Concept Publishing Company.

# 10

# Level of Empowerment of Respondents and Main Hindrances to Empowerment

After discussing in detail, the four variables which were selected to measure the level of empowerment of the rural women, it is now time to evaluate the general level of empowerment that has been achieved by the respondents of the present study. This evaluation will also help in either proving or disproving the two hypotheses that were formulated at the beginning of the study. The four variables that were considered as indices for empowerment were, political participation, decision-making ability, economic independence and access to basic facilities. These were selected because they are the basic elements of empowerment. A woman who has a high measure of these four variables is bound to be empowered. Among basic facilities education, health and nutrition were considered the most important. These are the facilities that have been included in HDI too, which is used by the UNDP for preparing the Human Development Report, for member nations every year. In this chapter besides discussing the level of empowerment, the hindrances women face in getting empowered will also be discussed.

Various authors have written about the powerlessness of women in traditional Indian society and the efforts to empower them in recent times. Kumar and Varghese write that there are three main reasons for women's powerlessness, the patriarchal system which gives a subordinate status to women, women's physiological make up which confines them to reproduction and household activities and various socio cultural factors which condition women to accept subordinate position and remain ignorant, less literate and less aware. Efforts have to be made to address all these factors, both those within and beyond the control of women, in order to give them their rightful place in society.[1] Jaya Arunachalam writes about the various road blocks to women's empowerment. She mentions the gender bias that operates at all levels, the neglect of the girl child, the feminisation of poverty in modern times, the ill effects of the process of globalization on workers in the unorganized sector [where 85% women work], the adverse effects of SAP on the very livelihood of the poor, the anti-poor policies of the Government on management of natural resources and the country's unfavourable macro economic balance which is threatening the process of empowerment that has been achieved by the poor. She has written how the Working Women's Forum has helped in empowering poor women through cooperative movement and trade unionism. She says the poor are excellent resources if reinforced with training inputs to become strong leaders in the community.[2] Samanta emphasizes the role of macro finance in empowering rural women while she concedes that it is a very comprehensive term which is a way of defining, challenging and overcoming barriers of one's life through which people increase their ability to shape their own lives and environment. Empowerment has to be in terms of information, knowledge, skills, awareness and it has to be against powerful forces of domination and exploitation.[3] Thus we see that for empowerment women need to acquire knowledge, have access to basic facilities, fight for their rights collectively, learn to take correct decisions, have control over resources and be able to shape their lives. They have to surmount various difficulties in order to achieve it.

The empowerment level of women in Uttaranchal is generally considered to be higher than that of women in other States according to available information and also according to women dignitaries of the State. This does not mean that women do not have problems. On the contrary hill women have too many problems to face in their daily life and also suffer from over work and poor health. It also does not mean that all the women in Uttaranchal are fully empowered. The level of empowerment varies from area to area and from one aspect to the other. For instance women are more active in public life and politics but their access to health services and nutrition is not satisfactory. Although female literacy rate is quite high in the State and it is one of the highest in the country for Dehradun district, rural women are not well educated. Their literacy rate in remote villages is not good. Most rural women are also bound by traditions and superstitions, specially in remote areas, but efforts to raise awareness are bearing fruit gradually. Women of the hills form the back bone of the economy and have some control over resources although in a patriarchal society, they do not own the land in their names. Dr Santosh Chauhan, who is the Chair-person of the Uttaranchal Mahila Aayog writes, 'Uttaranchal is poised to develop into a model State for women. Women, have always made their presence felt in every sphere of life in the State and have done it proud. To mark the International Women' Day, this year, [2006], thousands of women from different parts of the State, representing NGOs,

Mahila Mangal Dals, Self Help Groups and other social organizations converged on Dehradun at a function chaired by the Chief Minister, to renew their commitment to protection of women's rights.' On this occasion, the State minister for women empowerment and child welfare, Amrita Rawat said that the Centre has commended the exemplary work being done by the state in the field of women's empowerment. She said, 'Uttaranchal is the state where government has discriminated in favour of women on such a large scale to improve the quality of their life.'[4]

At a workshop organised by State Women's Commission in 2005, on Women Empowerment, Dr. Sudha Pande, the senior most member of Uttaranchal Public Service Commission said, 'Although women of Uttaranchal have always been brave, they have many problems which should be taken into account while formulating any policy for empowering them. The problems of hill women are different to those of the women of the plains. These include drudgery, poverty, lack of health facilities, mal nutrition and alcoholism of men.' Smt. Radha Raturi, Secretary, Social Welfare Department, Government of Uttaranchal says women play a very important role in the local economy in the state and form the backbone of rural life. It is essential that they have easy access to special development programmes, so that they can perform their role in a better way. Indira Mahila Samekit Vikas Yojna is an ambitious initiative by the State government to empower women. She noted that although women work very hard both at home and in the fields and form backbone of economy, they are subordinate to men in the patriarchal society with a feudal mind set. They are not able to take important decisions on their own. They have health problems. Their literacy rate is very low in remote villages. There are instances where daughters in law have committed suicide due to ill treatment.

She wanted to emphasize that hill women have many problems but continue to work hard as there is no other option. Since they work both at home and fields, mostly in the absence of men folk it is felt that they are empowered, but it is superficial empowerment. For real empowerment it is necessary that they get better access to health facilities, education, legal awareness and are not over burdened by work. They should have a say in family matters and property matters. All these statements show that while rural women in Garhwal play a very important role in society and economy, they also face too many problems in so doing. Since they are assets to their families, they enjoy a better status than rural women elsewhere but they continue to be subordinate to men, as in most other societies.[5]

The respondents of the present study too work very hard and play an important role in their families, fields and family occupation. Data have shown that they are quite satisfied with their condition since they are mostly consulted in important decisions and money matters and get reasonably good nutrition and health care. When questioned about the status of women in the families in their villages, they responded as follows :

**Table 47 : Distribution of Respondents by their View Regarding Status of Women in the Family**

| *S.No.* | *Categories* | *No. of Respondents 'a'* | *No. of Respondents 'b'* | *Percent* |
|---|---|---|---|---|
| 1. | Satisfactory | 76 | 67 | 71.5 |
| 2. | Unsatisfactory | 21 | 25 | 23 |
| 3. | Very bad | 3 | 8 | 5.5 |
| | Total | 100 | 100 | 100 |

Data show that 71.5 per cent respondents feel women have a satisfactory status in the family which is an encouraging response; 23 per cent feel it is not satisfactory which means women are not happy with the importance given to them. A small number, 5.5 per cent said women have a very bad status, which means they must be oppressed and ill treated. The positive response of the majority shows that these women have a satisfactory level of empowerment. The number of positive responses are higher for women of Raipur villages, indicating that they are more empowered than respondent of Doiwala villages.

Other indicators of a satisfactory level of empowerment included a good degree of political participation, sufficient decision making ability, nearly sufficient economic self reliance and not much gender discrimination in accessing facilities, as was shown in preceding chapters. On the other hand only 30 per cent respondents knew about women's rights, 48.5 per cent are illiterate and very few are benefiting through self help groups, adult literacy programme or vocational training programmes. Among the respondents only 9.5 per cent said they were members of Self help groups; 6.5 per cent said they go to adult literacy classes and 8 per cent said they knew about some special programmes being run by their Panchayats for women. Health care facilities are not adequate in small villages and for various health problems they have to go to private doctors or to the city, but the responses about use of facilities available at health centers were better than responses to adult literacy etc. since 30.5 per cent respondents said they go regularly to health centers. Some villages are better developed than others with regard to housing, cleanliness, educational facilities, efficient Panchayat and other facilities like shops, health center and water taps etc. Nawada is the most prosperous village, but a small village Kotla, which falls under Nawada Panchayat is quite backward. There is predominance of poor Muslim families in this village. Most of them are daily wage earners. The houses are small and dilapidated. The standard of life is very low. Badripur is a developed village. Other villages vary in their degree of development and prosperity. Markham Grant has some small villages like Banjara Basti which is very backward. Jolly Grant also has smaller villages which are semi-developed, with some very poor residents living in huts; but close by there were big houses of rich people. In Majri Grant, some families of Pal community, who sell milk are rich, while the labourers are poor. Hansuwala has many Muslim households who are quite prosperous and well educated. The daughters are studying in Colleges. Thus there is a variety of people in the sample villages and in the sample itself, who belong to different economic strata but in general it was found that women are not oppressed or exploited. They may be poor and uneducated but very few [5.5%] as shown above, indirectly complained of ill treatment. In fact these women do not tolerate oppression of even any other woman. This was illustrated by the following incident. The Mahila Mangal Dal in Nawada once rescued a girl of backward caste from her in laws' who used to torture her in village Bhanwala. Her husband was a cancer patient and very ill. The girl was afraid for her life. The members of the Dal went to her in laws' house and brought back the girl and her dowry The husband died after sometime and now she is remarried. In other villages women of Mahila Dals have helped to get daughters of poor parents married.

In Badripur women have made great economic progress by forming a Self Help Group under the president ship of Savita Devi. This group started a dairy and is doing good business. In Mothrowala too, a Self Help Group, named Prerna made good profits.

There are some women in these villages who have risen from destitute position to economically secure positions by their hard work and intelligence. Rukmini Joshi of Mothrowala is one such person. Sharmila Shahi, who works in an Aanganwadi in Navada is another woman who has made great progress in her profession and improved the standard of living of her family. Sarla Thapa, Pradhan of Nawada Panchayat has been doing social work for the last twenty years since she joined Mahila Mangal Dal. She was responsible for bringing electricity to some small villages and telephone line to Nawada. These are all examples of women's empowerment and it shows that some women have reached satisfactory level of empowerment and are inspiring others, in the sample villages.

Some questions were put to the respondents to find out their attitude towards various issues like dowry, age at marriage, divorce etc. Questions were also asked to find out their aspirations and their reasoning. Such information shows to what extent the women have changed positively in their outlook due to greater awareness and how much are they motivated to improve their lot in general. Motivation and awareness help in psychological empowerment of women, which is essential to build their confidence and make them successful in their efforts at improving their condition. Narasimhan has written that more than money, psychological empowerment makes women achieve their goals. Psychological empowerment means building of self confidence and getting rid of unnecessary fears and hesitation. She writes that an NGO named AWARE has been successful in motivating poor rural women to demand their rights and undertake projects to improve their economic condition.[6] The following tables show the responses of the women to different questions, which show their thinking.

**Table 48 : Distribution of Respondents by their Response to Whether Giving of Dowry is Correct**

| *S.No.* | *Categories* | *No. of Respondents 'a'* | *No. of Respondents 'b'* | *Percent* |
|---|---|---|---|---|
| 1. | It is correct | 27 | 26 | 26.5 |
| 2. | It is not correct | 73 | 74 | 73.5 |
| | Total | 100 | 100 | 100 |

More than one fourth of the respondents are in favour of the dowry system, although dowry has been proclaimed as a crime in our country. Thus their response is not right, but 73.5 per cent are not in favour of dowry which is a good response. Actually dowry continues to be given and taken in our country openly, specially among rich, educated and respectable families; therefore the response of 26.5 per cent respondents, although not correct, cannot be totally condemned. They feel that if they give dowry to their daughters they will be happy and respected in their husband's house. Secondly they feel the daughters have a right to some expensive gifts from parents because inspite of various laws, daughters are not given any share in father's property. Next they were asked whether they would like to take dowry for their sons. Once again a huge majority, 78.5 per cent said they would not like to take dowry for their sons, but 21.5 per cent said they would like to take it. Probably they feel that when they are forced to give dowry to their daughters then they should also be able to take it for their sons. That taking and giving of dowry is a crime is beside the point for them, because they see people following the dowry system openly.

They all knew that the dowry system has become a problem for most parents because the demands of the bridegroom's parents are becoming atrocious. So when they were asked to present some solutions to solve this problem, they came up with some options, which are shown in the next table.

**Table 49 : Distribution of Respondents by the Suggesstions they gave to Solve the Problem of Dowry**

| *S.No.* | *Solutions* | *No. of Respondents 'a'* | *No. of Respondents 'b'* |
|---|---|---|---|
| 1. | Refuse to take dowry | 72 | 50 |
| 2. | Refuse to give dowry | 34 | 48 |
| 3. | Inform police | 7 | 7 |
| 4. | Increase awareness | 14 | 16 |
| 5. | Make daughter self reliant | 5 | 7 |
| 6. | Promote inter caste marriage | 4 | 5 |

Most of them feel that the problem of dowry can be solved by refusing to take or give dowry and this is the best solution. Unless people themselves stop the practice law cannot put an end to it, specially when law enforcement is very lax in our country. Greater number of respondents from Raipur villages suggest that dowry should not be taken. This is the most positive step one can take to solve the problem. Very few feel informing the police will help and again this is also true, because police generally doesn't take serious action against the offenders. Unfortunately very few have said that making daughters self reliant will put an end to dowry problem. Actually this is the best way to overcome the problem of dowry but may be the villagers do not understand this yet, or may be it is not practical in their set up. Increasing awareness of people about the evils of dowry system, in an effective way, may also help in stopping it. A small number said inter caste marriages would solve the problem. This is true in the sense that generally inter caste marriage is a love marriage so when the boy and girl are willing to marry parents cannot demand dowry. But this is quite a revolutionary suggestion. When asked what they would do if their daughter is ill treated by in laws for dowry, only 1 per cent said they would give what is demanded and 95 per cent said they would protest and try to settle the issue by discussion and reasoning and 4 per cent said they would go to court. These responses show a high level of mental empowerment.

There were questions about age at marriage and divorce also which showed the attitude of the respondents. In India the minimum age for the marriage of a girl is 18 years and child marriage has been declared a crime but child marriages are performed in many communities and also in villages with out hesitation. When questioned about the right age for getting a daughter married the respondents gave the following answers :

**Table 50 : Distribution of Respondents by their View Regarding Right Age for Marriage of Daughter**

| *S.No.* | *Categories* | *No. of Respondents 'a'* | *No. of Respondents 'b'* | *Percent* |
|---|---|---|---|---|
| 1. | below 18 yrs | 6 | 9 | 7.5 |
| 2. | 18-20 yrs | 42 | 44 | 43 |
| 3. | above 20 yrs | 52 | 47 | 49.5 |
| | Total | 100 | 100 | 100 |

Nearly half the respondents feel the right age for marriage is above 20 years of age. This is a very modern and liberal view. Rural women generally want to get their daughters married as soon as possible to be free of a big responsibility but these rural women feel daughters should not be married when they are very young instead they should be given education and may be some vocational training so that they can earn a living if required. Most of the respondents said they want their daughters to get good education and they are sending them to schools and colleges for this purpose. These responses also show good sense and positive decision-making ability. It also shows their positive attitude towards the importance of education and economic independence for girls and women. It is generally noticed that poor women, whether rural or urban, who are not educated and who have led submissive lives, want their daughters to improve and achieve all that they themselves could not. Today more opportunities are also available so they want their daughters to avail of them. This is a very positive attitude which can bring about desirable change in women's status. The questions regarding divorce were related to triple Talaq among Muslims and the frequency of divorce among other religious groups. The respondents were asked whether they considered triple Talaq correct. This question was asked because there are quite a few Muslims in the sample and secondly because this issue has been discussed a lot recently. Many respondents did not know the meaning of this term. It is the custom of divorcing the wife by pronouncing the word Talaq three times at one sitting. Some Muslims say it is right while some do not. After the meaning was explained to the respondents, 25.5 per cent said it is right. This is a regressive view. Among these 25.5 per cent more than half were Muslims. They have been told by religious leaders that triple Talaq is correct so they feel it is right. About divorce among other religious groups 83.5 per cent said it is given occasionally but not very often and the rest said it is not given among Hindus. This again is a very traditional answer, dictated by religious belief that marriage is irrevocable. But many Hindu men desert their wives and in modern times there is provision for divorce in all religions in India. The majority of respondents gave positive responses which again shows that they are on the right path with regard to correct decision making.

This is the rosy side of the picture. On the other hand many women have not yet reached a satisfactory level of empowerment due to various hindrances and problems. Among the respondents there were many who were satisfied with their lot and felt their status was good but observation showed that there is scope for improvement. Generally women are socialized in such a way that they do not expect much for themselves, specially in their husband's house. They are not used to demanding any rights or comforts. Therefore if they are not ill treated and if they have a satisfactory married life they are fully satisfied; but in reality, they need better nutrition, better health care and more freedom to take their own decisions and participate in public life. For all these changes there has to be a drastic change in the outlook of the whole society. Even in cities women are not empowered to a satisfactory extent, mainly due to the traditional attitude towards women and their role. In fact often, women of lower economic status, whether in cities or villages, are forced by circumstances to be more independent in taking decisions and doing outside work. In the sample villages the main hindrances in women's empowerment were their lack of knowledge, their over worked condition, their poverty, their hesitation and fear of unknown. When asked about the acceptance of women working out side home or taking part in politics, a small percentage of respondents had answered in the negative. Similarly nearly half the respondents had said working outside home does not improve a woman's status. These responses show indirectly that their men folk do not like women to work outside home. This is a psychological hindrance to empowerment, which restrains women from going out either to work or to take part in politics There are many physical hindrances too.

Over work and drudgery are also responsible for rural women's apathy to go out and participate in community work or go for adult literacy classes, vocational training programme etc. When asked about their daily routine most respondents enumerated all the jobs they do at home, in the farms and in the nearby forest. Besides all the housework and child care, they take care of cattle, collect fire wood, make cow dung cakes and cut grass for cattle. Many of them work either in their own fields or as labourers in others' fields. Two questions were asked about who takes care of cattle and who brings fire wood to find out whether men help in these jobs. The answers are presented in the following tables.

**Table 51 : Distribution of Respondents by their Response to Question on Care of Cattle**

| *S.No.* | *Categories* | *No. of Respondents 'a'* | *No. of Respondents 'b'* | *Percent* |
|---|---|---|---|---|
| 1. | wife takes care | 21 | 42 | 31.5 |
| 2. | other women help | 10 | 26 | 18 |
| 3. | men take care | 3 | 19 | 11 |
| 4. | labourers take care | 0 | 10 | 5 |
| 5. | not applicable | 66 | 3 | 34.5 |
| | Total | 100 | 100 | 100 |

There is a great difference between the responses of the two groups because in Raipur villages very few people are occupied in dairy farming where as in Doiwala villages many people are engaged in it. The Pal community in these villages is engaged exclusively in this occupation. Therefore while only 3 per cent in Doiwala villages said they do not have cattle, 66% in the Raipur group of villages said they do not have cattle. The important point to note is that mostly women take care of cattle in all the villages. Labourers work only for rich families. Men take care in a small number.

Similarly the job of collecting fire wood and fuel is also done mostly by women, as is shown in the next table.

**Table 52 : Distribution of Respondents by their Response to Question on Collection of Fire Wood**

| S.No. | Categories | No. of Respondents 'a' | No. of Respondents 'b' | Percent |
|---|---|---|---|---|
| 1. | Done by men | 25 | 20 | 22.5 |
| 2. | Done by women | 65 | 69 | 67 |
| 3. | Not applicable | 10 | 11 | 10.5 |
| | Total | 100 | 100 | 100 |

Data show that 67 per cent respondents said that women go out to collect fire wood and fodder while 22.5 per cent said men do so. Even this is a big percentage of men, for collecting wood and fodder because generally women do this job exclusively. Luckily in the sample villages women do not have to trudge long distances to carry water. Water is available through taps and hand pumps in the villages. These data were presented just to show that women have to do a lot of work which is very time consuming and tiring not to show that women should not be doing them. Of course women have to do these jobs since men work at fields or at work place for most of the day and in the rural life style these jobs are essential. The solution is to improve life style so that fire wood and wood as fuel is not required and fodder for animals is easily available and for this economic status has to improve.

There are some more problems which the rural women face. These problems keep them occupied to such an extent that they do not find time for capacity building or any social activity. While visiting the villages it was noticed that for rural women going out to collect fire wood or to cut grass was itself a social occasion because many women gathered at some one's house and then left together in a convivial group towards the forest. Non-availability of many essential goods or difficulty in finding them in their village are the main problems of these women. In this regard two questions were asked, one about non-availability of goods and the other about problems about accessing basic facilities in day to day life. The following tables show the details.

**Table 53 : Distribution of Respondents by their Response to Non-Availability of Essential Goods in Village**

| *S.No.* | *Non available goods* | *No. of Respondents 'a'* | *No. of Respondents 'b'* |
|---|---|---|---|
| 1. | food items | 3 | 12 |
| 2. | medicines | 45 | 51 |
| 3. | clothes | 50 | 71 |
| 4. | utensils | 31 | 41 |
| 5. | women's accessories | 25 | 35 |
| 6. | stationery & books | 23 | 31 |

This table shows that medicines and good clothing are not easily available to many. The other items are also important for women and children and the desired things are not available to some. The standard of living in these villages, specially in the villages in Raipur block is improving and due to proximity to Dehradun, villagers too want to use latest fashionable clothes, accessories, food items, stationery etc. These are not available in villages, otherwise ordinary clothes, stationery and utensils etc. are available. Medicines are very important and the basic essential ones are available in medical stores in bigger villages but special prescriptions for some diseases and some tonics etc. may not be available. Non availability of various items required by women for themselves or for their children is also a hindrance to their empowerment because it prevents them from doing what they want and forces them to make compromises.

**Table 54 : Distribution of Respondents by their Response to Problems in Daily Life**

| S.No. | Problems | No. of Respondents 'a' | No. of Respondents 'b' |
|---|---|---|---|
| 1. | Problem of water | 31 | 26 |
| 2. | problem of electricity | 9 | 12 |
| 3. | problem of transport | 34 | 47 |
| 4. | waste disposal problem | 45 | 51 |

Data show that the biggest problems for these respondents are lack of good water supply, lack of proper transport facilities, lack of dust bins and some have the problem of no electricity connection. These problems are related to empowerment directly because they are restricting the women's access to basic facilities. In both the above tables the respondents from group 'b' i.e., Doiwala block villages seem to have more problems than the respondents from Raipur block villages. This is because the Raipur block villages are closer to Dehradun and are also more prosperous and developed than the Doiwala villages.

In the final analysis it can be said that while a majority of the respondents are satisfied with their status and participate in family decision making and also take an interest in political activities, their access to basic facilities has to improve and they should be motivated to a greater extent to become economically independent. The various hindrances and problems they face in their daily life probably restrain them from undertaking activities to improve their condition. If their education and awareness improves it will motivate them to improve. It is also necessary that their work load is reduced and their problems are solved. While others can provide help and guidance, the women themselves will have to find out ways and means to solve their problems. The government and Panchayat offer many facilities to women but many women are not aware of them or are not interested in them. They should benefit fully through the various schemes and facilities. Education, awareness generation and motivation are the main tools for encouraging these rural women to make efforts to empower them selves.

## References

1. Kumar H & Varghese J Women's Empowerment, 2005, Regency Publications.
2. Arunachalam Jaya Women's Equality-A Struggle for Survival, 2005, Gyan Publishing House.
3. Samanta R K Empowering Rural Women, 2005, The Women Press Delhi.
4. News Item in Times of India March 2006.
5. Interview of Smt Radha Raturi by Dr Zainab Rahman.
6. Narsimhan S [1999] Empowering Women Sage Publications.

# 11

# Rural Women of Kumaon and their Level of Empowerment

Having studied in detail about the level of empowerment of rural women in Garhwal villages, now we will examine the level of empowerment of rural women in Kumaon, on the basis of studies and field work of various authors and researchers. This chapter will present information of the activities and achievements of Kumaoni women.

Kumaon is the western sub region of Uttarakhand State It comprises of 5 districts, namely, Pithoragarh, Champavat, Almora, Bageshwar and Nainital. Udham Singh Nagar and Haridwar comprise the Terai region. Kumaon has a long history, which has been chronicled by Atkinson in Himalayan Gazetteer'. The present day "Baijnath-Garud" area in Bageshwar was known as Katyur. The remains of the ancient city of Kartikpur have been found here. The inscriptions on the walls of Bageshwar temple tell us about the ruling dynasties of Kartikpur. Basant Dev was the first ruler of Kartikpur. His dynasty was Katyuri Dynasty. After this dynasty many others, like the Chands of Champavat, Bams of Pithoragarh, Manikotis of Gangoli and Pals of Askot, ruled over Kumaon, between 1223 AD and 1545 AD. The Chand dynasty continued till the 18th century but it became weaker and in 1790, the Gorkha king Ran Bahadur attacked Kumaon and defeated the Chand ruler. The East India Company entered Kumaon in 1815, by defeating the Gorkhas Mr Trail was the first British administrator of the erstwhile Kumaon [Uttarakhand]. He tried to remove the Begaar System and developed the Mule Army. The people of Kumaon showed resistance to anti people policies of the British in the 19th century and raised their voice against the Press Act, Arms Act and Ilbert Bill of the British Government. There was a general opinion agaist Begaar and people struggled to remove it. In 1893, a bill against the Begaar System was passed by the Congress. The educated middle class of Kumaon set up many local asociations to create nationalism and spread awareness about atrocities of British. Finally in September 1916, the Kumaon Council came into existance, whos main objective was to find a solution to Uttarakhand's economic and social problems.[1]

Guha and Gadgil write in their book, Ecology and Equity, that the women of Kumaon have always been active in social movements, both during the British period and after independence. They give two instances where women of Kumaon have been actively involved in environmental and social movements. Kumaon has a long heritage of social movements and this was seen in the continuing struggle against unregulated mining. Social activists worked hard to form village level Sangharsh Samities in the affected areas. The Laxmi Ashram in Kausani was succesful in involving women in this movement, whose own domain is most adversely hit by mining. Hence women played a leading role in the protests, including Dharnas, fasts and Padyatras and forced several mines to close down. Similarly women of Kumaon played a significant role in proteting against state usurpation of forests in 1921. The widespread peasant movement virtually paralised the administration and the British were forced to withdraw control over less valuable forest areas.

This led to the formation of Van Panchayats. The Van Panchayats of the hill districts of Uttar Pradesh constituted the only major network of village forests mandated by law, in India. Under the Kumaon Panchayat forest rules of 1931, a Van Panchayat can be formed out of non-private land within the settlement boundaries of a village. Van Panchayats have the power to regulate the use of the forest by the villagers.[2]

Vandana Shiva writes about the Laxmi Ashram in Kausani and its work with the women of Kumaon. The Ashram was set up by Sarla Ben, a Gandhian, in the early 20s. She wanted to educate the hill women of Kumaon at this Ashram. Her full time committment was to make them realise that they were not beasts of burden but goddesses of wealth since they rear cattle and produce food performing 98% of all labour in farming and animal husbandry. One of the early women's movement started by these women in Uttarakhand was the anti-alcohol movement. Its aim was to control alcoholic addiction among men. For the women drunkenness meant violence. Women picketed at shops in Tehri and other places. In the 60s they demonstrated in Ghansyali. Finally prohibition came into effect in Tehri, Uttarkahi, Chamoli and Pithoragarh. The main idea of Sarla Ben was to empower the women.[3] Women of Kumaon joined their sisters from Garhwal in the Chipko Movement to save the forests. This movement was started in 1973 by the members of Dhasholi Gram Swarajya Mandal. The women of Laxmi Ahram also joined this movement and in 1975 the women started a 75 day trek from Uttar Kashi to Kausani to mobilise public opinion on women's increasing work load due to deforestation. In June 1977 a meeting of all the activists in the hills held in Silyara Ashram, further strengthened the movement and consolidated the resistance to commercial felling of trees.

Women of Kumaon have been active in politics too, both before and after Independence. In the Quit India movement of 1942 many women took part of whom some names are Durgawati Pant, Bhagirathi Devi Verma and Kunti Devi. The role of women in the Uttarakhand movement for the formation of a separate state in the 90s is very well known. They took part in Dharnas, protest rallies and Bandhs to put pressure on the Government and also courted arrest many times. During the Rampur Tiraha incident some women also lost their lives. Veena Pani Johi writes in detail about the role of women of Kumaon in various socio political movements. She writes women of Kumaon played an unforgettable role in anti alcohol movement when they got the liquor shops closed and the contracts for making and selling liquor cancelled. Women like Revati Uniyal, Tincturi Mai, Vimala Bahuguna, Tara Devi and Maini Devi did a lot to prevent the destruction caused by alcoholism to people, specially women. In village Khirakot of Almora women struggled from 1978-1982 in order to stop the mining of limestone being carried out by Katiyar Mineral Company. They had to fight a long battle and even go to court but finally they were successful in preventing their green village from becoming a desert. In Kotdwar women from Kumaon and Garhwal played a prominent role in the landless farmers movement. Radha Bhatt of Laxmi Ashram has taken part in many movements for the welfare of the hill people and also provided effective leadership and direction to them. She continues her good work with total dedication to this day. Women of the hills have courted arrest with small children accompanying them during the Satyagraha movement in British rule.[4]

After acquainting ourselves with the potential and achievements of the women of Kumaon, now we will see what steps the Uttar Pradesh and then the Uttaranchal Govt. took to improve their condition and to empower them. The Khadi and Village Industry Commission, KVIC, has tried to involve rural women in science and technology programmes in order to reduce their burden and help them work more efficiently, for instance use of innovations in spinning, weaving and in grinding and use of improved furnace and boiling pan and use of gobar gas etc. These programmes were also implemented in Himalayan region.[5] The projects like DWCRA, MSY and IMY were also implemented in this region in the 80s and 90s.

The Watershed Management Programme was also implemented in the hill region of UP. It still being implemented in the new state. Under the Watershed Management Programme various schemes are implemented for rural development and also empowerment of women. Many studies have been conducted to find out the benefits that have accrued to the rural women by these schemes. One such study has been made of the IWDP Shiwalik [Hills II] which covers the rural areas of the Districts Pauri, Nainital and Uddhamsingh Nagar. The objective of this Project is productivity enhancement of the area through sustainable development of natural resources and improvement in the economic condition of communities with their active participation. The project area is characterized by subsistence agriculture due to fragmented, small and unconsolidated holdings, dependence on rain and low productivity. Due to this there is large male migration placing a burden on women. Although women make a tremendous contribution to agriculture their work is under valued and remains non-monetised. Secondly, deforestation has also increased the work load of rural women. It was felt that women should be given importance in development schemes as they are the main stake holders. Thus the Project focuses on women and aims at strengthening them through capacity building, providing employment and entrepreneurship opportunities, reducing drudgery and establishing linkages. For this purpose Self Help Groups were formed for women. These groups provide a platform for women as well as function as credit and thrift groups. Women meet in these groups and discuss their problems and try to solve them. Most of the SHGs now have substantial savings and have started inter loaning activity. The following table shows the status of the SHGs under this Project upto Dec.2003.

**Table : Status of Self Help Groups (Upto Dec. 2003)**

| *Division* | *No. of SHGs* | *Saving amount Rs.* | *Amount of inter-loaning in Rs.* |
|---|---|---|---|
| Kotdwar | 136 | 704144 | 22000 |
| Lansdown | 113 | 685668 | 206350 |
| Rishikeh | 115 | 569064 | 23130 |
| Haldwani | 77 | 722111 | 971500 |
| Ramnagar | 55 | 349885 | 164450 |
| TOTAL | 496 | 3030872 | 1387430 |

*Source* : Watershed Management Directorate Uttaranchal.

The table shows that the SHGs in the scheme are quite successful in their functioning. Income generation activities were also generated in the SHGs like fruit preservation and processing, candle making, handicrafts and vegetable cultivation. There are some NGOs which market these products through outlets in cities. The self help groups are also encouraged to connect with local markets to sell their produce. The women are educated and trained to be self reliant and more professional in their work. The study concludes that positive results have been noticed in the social, political and economic lives of the women who are members of these SHGs and there has been capacity development too. These women have improved their standard of living, are more aware, articulate and confident and are participating actively in local politics. All this shows that their level of empowerment has risen.[6]

There are some studies of women of Kumaon showing their condition, their problems, their level of political participation etc. Pande and Singh have made a study of the tough life these women lead. They write that these women play a very prominent role in the regional economy by their hard work both at home and in fields. The hill women's expeditions to the forests on a daily basis are no less demanding than the success of Bachendri Pal in climbing Mount Everest. Thousands of Kumaoni women travel daily from their kitchen to the forest since their early childhood to their old age to collect fuel, fodder and water. Today due to shrinking of forest they have to travel greater distances which has many types of adverse effects on their lives. The factors that are responsible for increasing the burden of these women are the social set up which compels women to arrange for fuel, the increasing population creating greater demand for fuel, the decreasing forest cover, lack of any alternative solution to fuel problem in rural Himalayas and illiteracy and orthodoxy of village folk. Walking long distances and then working for four to five hours in ill lighted and poorly ventilated kitchens has bad effect on the health of these women.[7] Two studies related to political participation of rural women in Nainital district show that although women in the rural areas of Nainital have started taking part in Panchayat elections, they are not taking independent decisions. They are generally guided by their men folk. In order to empower them truly, social inequalities should be removed and hindrances in women's freedom should be eliminated. In this connection, Dr Mahipal writes, women in Uttaranchal are largely educated and assertive but assessment of the working of Panchayats in the state shows that people's aspirations in terms of becoming participators in decision making in decentralized governance, planning and development have not yet been fulfilled completely. Women should have a greater role in all these processes.

The NGOs are also doing commendable work in empowering women in the Kumaon region. Some NGOs are working with women in agriculture while some are helping them to become economically independent through entrepreneurship and capacity building. Sahyog is an NGO working in Almora district to increase the awareness of rural women and also to highlight their contribution to agriculture. One of its recent studies revealed that women, young and old, knew more about traditional seed varieties and agricultural practices, than men folk. The illiterate women ranked and stored seed varieties on the basis of criteria like soil type, need for irrigation, yield, taste and nutrition. Now they are breaking the male bastion of using the plough too.[8]

Gyanendra Pandey writes that women of Kumaon work from predawn to dusk and also in the night to complete all their duties and there is no other option for them but to follow this tough routine. Recently of course some change has been noticed in the attitude and work load of these women thanks to the interventions of some voluntary organizations. The Himalayan Study Centre based in Pithoragarh with branches in Gochar, Barakot, Someshwar and Bageshwar is an NGO which is active in creating awareness among rural women and encouraging them to demand their rights openly. It has presented a draft policy paper to the government through the NCW laying stress on involving women of the area in all development activities in the hills, because women are the major performers. The Centre is speeding up development work in Uttarakhand by encouraging agro-crafts, spreading awareness among women, ensuring women's participation in development work and organizing women into groups to discuss their problems and take action. The Centre has also encouraged and organized annual craft fair and Women's conference at Gochar. This has led to development of local crafts. It not only helps in marketing agricultural produce and handicrafts but also gives an opportunity for exchange of cultural programmes. The women from far flung areas meet at the Conference and collective issues are discussed and joint action planned. In the last conference 800 women representatives from Munsyari, Didihat, Berinag and Kanalicheena blocks participated. They discussed gender equality and protested against exploitation of women. The main discussion was on the topic of putting pressure on government to start women-oriented development programmes. Dr Dinesh Joshi, founder Director of the Centre says efforts made during last 15 years to empower women have started bearing fruit. Various programmes about awareness campaign, run by UN and International Women's Conference are being run at village level. The Centre is also organizing Panchayati Raj training, legal training, technology transfer and decentralization in agriculture schemes. It has successfully organized centers for resource management, informal education, Balwadi, Primary education, community education and micro level planning training and resource centers.[9]

In conclusion we can say that the rural women of Kumaon are trying to empower themselves by forming self help groups and also by participating in the political process. They have a long history of struggle against exploitation and deprivation, be it through a social movement or an ecological movement. On the basis of the information available from various studies it can be stated that the level of empowerment of these women is quite satisfactory with regard to political participation and decision making capacity and is improving with regard to economic independence with the formation of SHGs and with entrepreneurship efforts. The government as well as NGOs are helping and supporting the efforts of the rural women to empower themselves. Access to basic facilities may not be very satisfactory due to poverty and also due to remoteness of villages. There does not appear to be much gender discrimination in access to facilities because women are quite aware and assertive, but the normal bias towards male superiority which is all pervasive in Indian society, is also present in the hills. Women in the hills have a better status than women in the plains, mainly because they play a more important role in the economy and in community affairs than do women in the plains.

## References


1. Ekta Uniyal 2003 The Study of Uttaranchal Mentor.
2. Guha & Gadgil 1995 Ecology and Equity Penguin Books.
3. Shiva Vandana 1988 Staying Alive Kali for Women.
4. Joshi Veena Pani Him Aoj Trimonthly magazine Oct-Dec 2004.
5. Bahuguna Anjali [Ed] Science and Technology in relation to Rural Women 1990 Haranand Publication.
6. Project Report of Watershed Management Programme.
7. Rahman Zainab 2005 Women and Society Kalpaz Publications.
8. Rahman Zainab 2005 Women and Society Kalpaz Publications.
9. Ekta Uniyal 2003 The Study of Uttaranchal Mentor.

# 12

# Conclusion

This chapter will present the final conclusions of the project and try to show how far the two hypotheses have been proved or disproved. As mentioned many times in previous chapters, the level of empowerment of rural women in the sample villages was to be measured by studying four important variables which influence empowerment. These are political participation, decision-making power, economic independence and access to basic facilities like pure drinking water, health, education and nutrition. The two hypotheses framed in the second chapter were as follows :

1. Rural women in Garhwal participate in politics and decision making processes to a satisfactory extent.

2. Access to basic facilities and economic independence may not be available to a satisfactory extent due to various ground realities as well as traditional social set up.

The four variables were dealt with, in detail in four separate chapters and the previous chapter gave an over view of the level of empowerment in general and also pointed out the various hindrances which prevent many of the rural women from attaining a satisfactory level of empowerment. Now the two hypotheses will be discussed in detail, separately, quoting extensively from the relevant chapters, in order to find out how far these hypotheses have been proved or disproved.

The first hypothesis is related to political participation and decision making process, hence data regarding these two variables will be presented to prove the point. With regard to political participation it was noted in Chapter VI that 78.5 per cent respondents were involved in political activities to varying extents, while 21.5% were apathetic to politics. The categories of political participation used were those given by Lester Milbrath. Of the 78.5% respondents, 51% were involved in spectator activity, i.e., Voting and discussing politics; 19% were involved in transitional activity i.e., attending political meetings and contributing to political party funds and 8.5% were involved in gladiatorial activity i.e., holding party posts and Panchayat posts. This shows that political participation of the sample is quite satisfactory since the percentage of women who said they vote is higher than the percentage for the entire country, which was highest in 1984 election at 68.17%.[1] Political participation of women is quite low all over the world because politics is generally considered a male occupation. Considering this attitude, we find that women in the present sample take part in politics in good numbers. Keeping the above attitude in mind, the respondents were asked whether it was considered good for women to take part in politics and 61% replied in the affirmative. This also shows that the environment in the sample villages is very conducive for women's participation in politics. Generally politics is not considered a suitable activity for women, therefore very few women take part in it. But in the villages, after the 73rd Amendment 33 per cent seats were reserved for women candidates in Panchayat elections and the men folk see this as a good opportunity to capture power by encouraging their women to contest these reserved seats. Therefore women's participation in politics is now acceptable to most people.

While many rural women are active in politics now, quite a few of them do not know much and act as told by their husbands. This is not a healthy sign as it shows that their political empowerment is not real, but gradually women are learning to do things on their own. When asked whether women members of Panchayat took decisions on their own or obeyed the decisions of their husbands, 72 per cent respondents said that women take their own decisions, and on being asked about effectiveness of women Pradhans, 50 per cent said they were effective. During data collection and interviews with villagers it was found that while some women Pradhans are led by their husbands totally, some others are very independent and take decisions on their own. They are quite effective and popular too. One such Pradhan was Sarla Thapa of Navada village who has won from a general seat after contesting with men in the elections. The Pradhan of Badripur is also a woman and she also works on her own. On the other hand the Pradhan of Markham Grant was said to be led completely by her husband in her work. In Bhaniyawala also the Pradhan is a woman but all the work is done by her husband. This shows that women have to learn about the functioning of the Panchayat and understand their roles and their powers in order to perform their duties effectively on their own. The NGO Samarpit runs training classes for women members of Panchayat so that they can perform better. The researcher visited the other blocks falling in Dehradun district, namely Sahaspur, Vikasnagar, Kalsi and Chakrata to meet some Pradhans and other Panchayat members in the villages in these blocks to find out how they compare with the members in the sample villages. In Sahaspur the Pradhan is a woman, who said that she took some decisions on her own and took her husband's advice in taking some other decisions. In some other villages there were male Pradhans but they said that women were active in politics and there were women members in all Panchayats and women also run NGOs like Disha, which work for women's rights.

Some questions were put to the respondents to find out their awareness level and also their knowledge about empowerment. For instance they were asked what all should be done to empower women : 54% said women should be educated, 50.5% said they should become economically independent, 25.5% said their awareness should increase, 18% said their self confidence should increase and only 7.5% said they should get political power. Very few [5%] said they should be given their rights. These answers show a maturity of thinking which is rare among uneducated women. They know that one has to work hard to be empowered; not by just demanding rights. Roseanne Barr has said the same thing in her writing, 'No body gives you power you just take it.' They also understand that not every one can get political power, therefore a small number mentioned it, whereas education and economic independence are necessary for all women to achieve real empowerment. Another question was about knowledge of special facilities for women. Only 24 per cent respondents said they are aware of special facilities for women but 63 per cent said that if they come to know of these facilities they will be allowed to benefit through them by their men folk. While the percentage of women who know about facilities is low it is heartening that a big number wants to avail of them and feels that there would be no hindrance in availing of these facilities. This shows the women in the sample villages want to improve and have enough freedom to make efforts to improve their condition. Since political status of women is reflected by the extent of freedom granted to women with regard to their participation in political activity, it can be concluded, on the basis of above data, that women in the sample villages have a satisfactory level of political participation.

Political participation also entails decision-making, therefore the ability of taking good decisions was clubbed with political participation in the first hypothesis. Decision making is an important tool of empowerment. Women who can take correct decisions independently are truly empowered. Rural women are generally not allowed to take their own decisions, although they are mostly consulted before decisions are taken by men; but with women participating in politics through the Panchayats, they have also started taking their own decisions. Many women Pradhans have proved that they can take good decisions and implement them to promote welfare and progress. On the other hand many women Pradhans follow the decisions of their husbands. This does not prove that they are not capable of taking decisions on their own, but they are used to obey their husbands and not assert themselves. Women have to be motivated to use their reasoning power for decision making and to assert themselves to get their decisions accepted. Of course good reasoning requires intelligence. Education and awareness increase intelligence. In the rural set up very often experience improves intelligence. Many illiterate women are competent enough to take correct decisions regarding the welfare of the villagers because of their vast experience of rural life. It was found that in the present sample, 73 per cent respondents are consulted by their husbands in taking important decisions and 75.5 per cent are consulted in money matters. This shows that women are given importance in decision making process, be it of financial nature or social nature. More than a third of the respondents, [35%] said they are allowed to take important decisions independently. This shows that these women have proved their good sense to family members, who are confident that their decisions would be correct. All these data show that women in the sample participate in decision making process to a satisfactory extent. Besides this, the respondents were asked many questions to test their ability to take good decisions and their power of correct judgement They were asked whether women should go out to work with men in different occupations and 86 per cent said they should. When questioned about status of women today, 88 per cent said it is better now. Among the factors responsible for this improvement, the most important for them was greater independence, [53.5%] followed by employment [27%] and freedom to go out [26%] . These answers show that the respondents are very practical in their thinking and have given good replies. On the basis of all the data presented above regarding the respondents' political participation and participation in decision making process, it can be concluded that the first hypothesis has been proved correct and these rural women take part to a satisfactory extent in politics and decision making process.

The second hypothesis is related to the economic independence of rural women and their access to basic facilities. These variables were dealt with in Chapters VIII and IX. With regard to access to drinking water, 33.3% said they are fully satisfied and 46.5% said they are not highly satisfied because running water is not available always in the taps. When there is shortage of water in almost all cities, one cannot expect to have running water always. Thus in effect 80% respondents have satisfactory access to drinking water and 20% said water supply was bad. These respondents were mostly the ones who do not get their water from taps but from hand pumps and wells. The main source of water for household purpose was the tap [79%] while 17.5% use water from hand pumps and 3.5% from wells. Thus it can be said that access to water is satisfactory, but access to other facilities like healthcare and nutrition is not very satisfactory, as shown by data. When asked about the presence of Primary Health Centres in the villages only 52.5% respondents said there are Health Centres in their village. This may not be very true because there is a Health Centre in almost every village but some do not function regularly or efficiently so many villagers do not visit them instead they go to private doctors. Only 30.5% respondents said they go regularly to the health center for medicines etc. This shows that although the facility is available it is not being used by villagers, either because it does not satisfy their needs or because it is not provided properly. Some health centers like the one in Mothrowala are very old and function regularly, while some others do not function regularly. Besides the health centers there are also Aanganwadis where small children, young girls and pregnant and lactating mothers are provided some medical facilities like immunization, vitamins, iron capsules and iodised salt.

Regarding nutrition it was found that 69% respondents said they got good food to eat, but in reality their food is not really nutritious. In villages people are used to eating more of cereals and less of other food items like pulses, vegetables, and protein rich foods, specially the women do not get these food items in sufficient amounts. This is the trend in urban families also, because of patriarchal norms. Lack of knowledge of nutritious foods and their importance in good health and in prevention of diseases is also a factor, specially in villages. Women have to be made aware of importance of good nutrition and how it can be provided with out much expenditure. They have also to be taught how to cut, clean and cook vegetables in order to retain their nutrition value as much as possible. They have to be told what simple steps should be taken to prevent diseases and also how to handle common health problems of children. The mass media and NGOs are spreading awareness but there is need to work on a personalized basis.

In the sample 43.5% respondents said they have milch cattle at home so it can be assumed that they get sufficient amount of milk, at least for children, but the others may find it difficult to buy enough milk for all family members. Vegetables are grown at home by 35% respondents so it can be assumed they eat enough vegetables. Of the total sample 42% said they eat non-vegetarian food, nearly half of them are Muslims. Many of them take non vegetarian food occasionally, only few take it very often From rural standards in our country, it can be said that their nutrition is not bad although it is not ideal, but it was noticed in the villages that there were some very poor people who appeared really under nourished. Such people have to be helped in which-ever way possible to get better food. It is very sad that villagers who provide food to the whole country should remain under nourished themselves.

Access to facilities like adult literacy, vocational training, special programmes for women, is not satisfactory. The most important reason for this is the apathy of rural women. They are generally not interested in learning new skills, be it reading or stitching. They are keen that their daughters get good education and vocational training but they feel they are too old to learn or say they have no time Of course there are some exceptions.

With regard to economic independence the data show that 36% respondents said that they have access to personal income, either through wages or selling handicrafts etc., but most of them earn less than 1000 rupees per month. Nearly all of them said they spend it on children and family needs. A majority of the respondents [75.5%] are satisfied that they are consulted in money matters and 69% are allowed to spend money on their own although they do not earn money. Although the respondents seem satisfied there is need for them to achieve economic independence in the true sense by earning money through employment or entrepreneurship. Today there are many opportunities for rural women to start their own business or find employment. They should avail of these opportunities. One avenue available is the setting up of Self Help Groups. These are being encouraged by the Government and Banks are ready to give loans to women. In the present sample only 8.5% respondents said they are members of Self Help Groups. The researcher found out that only a few groups have been successful in running their business and making profits. Several groups have been discontinued because the members took loans and did not return or because the members could not make profits through their activities. Thus there is need for capacity building through vocational training and also of motivation and encouragement from the authorities, Panchayat members and social workers. The NGOs in the area, like Samarpit and Koshish are doing a good job by imparting training to women and helping them sell the finished products, but more efforts are required. Economic independence improves the status of the women in their families and also gives them greater role in decision-making process. Secondly it increases the self-confidence of the women and makes them more dignified. There are various examples of rural women benefiting through self help groups and micro finance not only in India but in other countries as well. Now it is well known how successful the Nobel Laureate Mohd. Yunus of Bangladesh has been in empowering poor rural women through his Grameen Bank. In India too there are many similar success stories. A news item in The Times of India proclaims the success of rural women from Kurnool District of Andhra Pradesh, with the caption, 'Rich-hearted poor women share new prosperity mantra.' These poorest of the poor women from villages of Orvakal Mandal have saved one rupee every day from their earnings for the last ten years and pooled their savings to set up a bank from which they lent money for various needs of villagers. Now the annual turn over of this mandal bank is Rs.15 crore. These women are being invited by many States like Bihar, Uttar Pradesh, Tamil Nadu and West Bengal to teach the poorest of the poor women there to function through Self Help Groups and fight against poverty.[2] In remote villages of Garhwal too rural women have achieved great success through Self Help Groups and one such group raised enough money to build a bridge across the river running through their village to help all villagers. With such examples available, it becomes obvious that the respondents have not made enough efforts to benefit through micro finance. They need to be assisted and motivated in order to make their ventures successful, like the group Prerna started by Rukmini Joshi in Mothrowala, was helped by Panchayat members and NGO workers and its members benefited through it. In the light of available data the conclusion regarding the second hypothesis is that the access to basic facilities and level of economic independence is not very satisfactory among the respondents and should improve. Thus the second hypothesis has also been proved correct, although this unsatisfactory condition is more because of ignorance and poverty rather than high level of gender discrimination. In the hypothesis it was said that the unsatisfactory levels may be due to ground realities and social set up and it has been found that ground realities are more responsible than social setup. Of course in a patriarchal society women are given less importance than men but in the sample the women seemed to be treated well and also reported so. It was also reported earlier that there is very little gender discrimination in treating male and female children. Among the older people too, there isn't much gender discrimination but women themselves do not assert their right to better facilities. Thus there is need to educate women about their requirements of proper nutrition and health care and stress its importance.

It is a fact that all over India, women specially poor women, do not have proper access to health services, nutrition and other basic facilities. Poverty as well attitude towards women and gender discrimination are responsible for it.

Various authors have written about this unsatisfactory condition. AR Saiyed writes that mortality rate is higher for females than males, in India. Nutritional inadequacies are also greater among females. Although there is higher morbidity among female children, attendance records of OPDs and clinics show preponderance of male children.[3] Similarly Kumar and Varghese write, 'In the utilization of health services women are always at a disadvantageous position. Health of women is least taken care of. In terms of food intake, women suffer worse deprivation intra familially. Women eat last at home and do without food if there is any shortage, as men and children are fed first.'[4] These writings support the findings of the present research; but with regard to economic independence, as mentioned earlier, unlike the respondents, rural women in different parts of the country are benefiting through micro finance projects.

The researcher would now like to present the findings of two international reports regarding the development that has taken place in the areas of education, nutrition, health services, economic independence and political participation of women in India in recent times.

The Human Development Report 2006 was released by UNDP in November 2006, India ranks 126 in the human development index [HDI] among 177 nations. It is placed in the lower half of 'medium human development' countries. HDI tracks human welfare as opposed to material wealth which is measured by GDP. It is a measure based on three dimensions of human development : life expectancy, literacy and standard of living. India's showing on all three counts is far from inspiring. The health expenditure of the state was 1.2 per cent of GDP and on education was 3.3 per cent of GDP. The Report also shows that improvement in the HDI has slowed down in the period 1990 to 2004 compared to the pace in the previous 15 years. Between 1975 and 1990 the

HDI score improved by 25% and in the next 14 years that figure has come down to 18.6%. This latter period coincides with the post reforms period when liberalization, privatization and globalization spread in Indian economy. The Report shows that India is one of the few countries which spends least on public healthcare. India's immunization rate for those who are one year old against measles is worst in the world.[5]

The World Economic Forum has also published its Global Gender Gap Report 2006, a survey of 115 world economies. It ranks India at 20th position, way ahead of some advanced nations like the US and Japan, in empowering women politically. In India 8 per cent women are in Parliament and 3 per cent occupy ministerial posts. While the US has greater percentage of women in both these categories, it has been placed in 66th spot because unlike India, the US never had any female leadership in the executive offices. But India is virtually at the bottom of the table when it comes to participation of women in the economy, their educational attainment and their health. The Global Gender Gap Index which measures the difference between the sexes in matters of economic participation and opportunity, educational attainment, health and survival and political empowerment, places India in 98th spot, since India's performance in all these areas except political empowerment is dismal. One statistical figure which shows the poor condition of health services for women in India is that 58% child births in India happen without any 'skilled' health staff to attend to. This is much higher than the percentage of such child births in the worst performing nations on the Index, for instance the percentage for Saudi Arabia is 9%.[6]

Both these reports confirm the findings of the present study.

Finally one comes to the conclusion that although a lot is being done in our country to improve the condition and status of women in general and rural women in particular, a lot more needs to be done to provide basic facilities to all, including the poorest of the poor, both in cities and in villages. Many NGOs and women's organizations are working relentlessly with the poor rural women to educate and motivate them so that they may make efforts to improve their condition. Women's Study Centres all over the country are also doing the important job of preparing a database about the condition and requirements of rural women; conducting research regarding rural women; creating awareness about the problems of women, both urban and rural in various ways and preparing competent activists and researchers for working in the cause of women. The researcher visited the Centre for Women's Studies, at AMU Aligarh and talked to the counsellor there who said that she runs an NGO for rural women and also gives advice to all those who come for it to the center. The Centre for Women's Studies and Development at BHU Varanasi was another center which the researcher visited. She found good resource material there about women's issues. This Centre has been holding Annual Refresher Courses in Women's Studies for university and college teachers. The Government has accepted in its National Education policy that Women's Studies are crucial to women's development because it is a critical input to promote better understanding of women's contribution to social processes, their struggles and aspirations and the conceptual obstacles that make them invisible. The Centre for Women's Development Studies in New Delhi is a premier institution which provides extensive reading material on women's issues. It carries on research work as well as undertakes awareness creating activities. At present this center is creating awareness about women's lives and activities through an excellent photo exhibition that has been curated by its members. The members are traveling with this exhibition to different cities to increase people's awareness. The researcher organized the display of this exhibition at her college in Dehradun.

The researcher also visited the National Institute of Rural Development in Hyderabad to find out about the various activities of this apex organization under the Ministry of Rural Development, Government of India. The organization offers training to more than 4000 senior level administrators, planners and rural development functionaries every year. It provides training, research, action research and consultancy in rural development. There is a Centre for Gender Studies at the NIRD which is headed by Dr. [Mrs] Mumtaz Taha. She said the rural women in Andhra Pradesh are better off than rural women in Northern States like UP and Bihar, mainly because the micro credit projects are being run efficiently in a disciplined way and there is little corruption. But she also said that women every where are considered subordinate to men and are not given equal importance in the family. This is something they have to cope with in their own way. This center designs and conducts training, research and consultancy activities on gender and development of women. Its thrust areas are : Gender sensitization, gender mainstreaming, gender budgeting and audit, gender in human settlement, women's empowerment, integrating gender into development projects, reproductive health, development of girl child and capacity building-gender training. At all these centers valuable data regarding Indian women, both rural and urban is being collected by research work and compiled systematically. Refresher courses in Women's Studies are being held and the resource material is also being published. In this way these centers are contributing to knowledge about Indian women, their achievements, aspirations, problems as well as their strengths and potential and their weaknesses. All this helps in increasing awareness about women's issues among women themselves as well as the society in general. This brings the women's agenda to the forefront.

Besides creating awareness among women and society in general about women's issues, it is also necessary to motivate women, specially the uneducated poor rural women, to improve their lot. For this purpose, educated women, social workers and academia should contact the rural women personally and talk to them; try to build their self confidence and self respect by appreciating their hard work and devotion to the family. They have to be told about the achievements of other rural women in other parts of the country so that they make an effort to realize their own potential. Awareness rallies and community gatherings should be held on regular basis to increase the knowledge of rural women.

The researcher held an awareness rally in one of the sample villages, namely Mothrowala, to educate the women about their rights and their potential. The field workers and post graduate research students took an active part in mixing with the rural women and young girls and talking to them about importance of education, health and hygiene, nutritious food and so on. Stress was laid on the importance of capacity building in the form of some vocational training or handicraft for achieving economic independence and being empowered. It was also stressed that emotional strength and self-confidence is necessary for empowerment and also a strong will and desire to be empowered. Easy to read books on legal literacy were distributed among them and various relevant laws were explained to them. The rural women belonged to low-income group and the younger among them were literate, but it was heartening to note that all the young girls between the ages of eight years to twenty years were attending schools and colleges. They were keen to do well in studies and also to learn some skill in order to earn. The interaction was very beneficial to both parties. It showed that the rural women and girls are eager to learn and improve their lot. This is the first step in the direction of empowerment.

Empowerment of women has been taken up in a big way in our country and the ninth and tenth Five Year Plans have chalked out the strategy for it in great detail, as described in an earlier chapter. Rural women are getting empowered mainly through political participation and economic independence. The Eastern Anthropologist has dedicated a volume to rural studies entitled, Rural Profiles : Scenario 2005. Eminent scholars have written in it about various changes that are taking place in villages and also stress that today NGOs are playing an important role in development of rural people. There is an article about empowerment of rural women in Adilabad District of Andhra Pradesh. The study shows that the tribal women were able to empower themselves through formation of Self Help Groups and Community Forest Protection Groups. They were helped by a conscientious government official in achieving success but after his transfer, they faced difficulties. This shows that if there is proper implementation of programmes for community development and if efficient supervision is available then empowerment of rural people, specially women, is possible.[7]

In the words of our President APJ Abdul Kalam, 'Empowerment of women is a must. Women's thoughts, their way of working and value systems will lead to faster development of a good family, good society and ultimately a good nation.' Addressing the Summit of the Powerless, in November 2006 in New Delhi, Dr. Kalam said employment generation coupled with skill-oriented education and training was the first step to empower the people of the nation.[8]

Thus the need of the hour is to motivate and help the poor rural women, who are the most exploited and discriminated section of society, to empower themselves. The government, the NGOs and individual activists are making commendable efforts and the target group is responding gradually in a positive way. With greater efforts on the part of all, gender justice and gender equality will become a reality when the poor women will be able to shape their own lives. This study has pointed out the strengths and the weaknesses of rural women in the sample, so that efforts may be made to encourage the strong points and remedy the weaknesses. It can be of help to planners and social activists who are involved with developmental work in this area.

## References

1. Rahman Zainab Women and Society, 2005, Kalpaz Publications.
2. News Item The Times of India, November 2006.
3. Anjum Mohini Muslim Women in India, 1992, Radiant Publishers.
4. Kumar H & Varghese J Women's Empowerment, 2005, Regency Publishers.
5. The Time of India News Item, 11th November 2006.
6. The Times of India News Item 4th December 2006.
7. The Eastern Anthropologist Rural Profiles : Scenario 2005, Vol. 58 Nos. 3, 4 July-December 2005.
8. The Times of India New Item, 21st November 2006.

# 13

# Case Studies

**Sharmila Shahi**

In the village of Navada, almost every one knows Sharmila Shahi, who is respected for her hard work and her achievements. During the field work the researcher and her data collectors came in contact with her many times and found her very cooperative and helpful in providing various type of information.

She is in her early thirties and has been married for twelve years. She had studied upto 10th standard when she got married and came to Navada. Her husband is a truck driver. She has two children aged eleven and nine years. Eight years back she decided to get herself enrolled for a training programme to work in Aanganwadi. She had the full support of her husband. Since her children were very small then she managed to complete the training with difficulty. On completion she started working in the Aanganwadi in Navada. In these eight years she has undergone two more trainings and is now the senior Aanganwadi worker with another woman as her helper. She has multi-farious duties to perform which include involving rural women in various programmes being run by the Aanganwadi, providing services like supplementary nutrition, health care and immunization to children below 6 years of age, adolescent girls, pregnant and lactating mothers, educating these women and girls about health and nutrition and providing pre-school education to children below 6 years of age. She has to maintain all records and take care of all the belongings of Aanganwadi. Her helper goes to the houses of young children in the morning to bring them to Aanganwadi. She also cooks food for children and Sharmila supervises her work.

Sharmila is very happy with her work and her family life. She says that working in the Aanganwadi has increased her knowledge and made her self-confident. Her trainings have helped increase her awareness and skills and this helps her in improving her own life as well as that of her children. Her employment has improved her standard of living. Now she has built a pucca house with a proper kitchen and bathroom. She has a Television and a fridge at home. She keeps her home very neat and clean. She has planted flowering plants in front of her house and keeps the area clean. Her son and daughter study in an English medium school. Her husband has recently bought a scooty for her which she has learnt to ride. It helps her in making trips to head office and training centre etc. Thus her initiative and hard work has helped improve the lives of all family members and she is very happy that she decided to work.

She is a person full of initiative. Besides working in the Aanganwadi, she had also started a Self Help Group for poor women with the help of the Panchayat. There were 10 members and the main activity was lending small loans to members on a small interest of 2% but it was not very successful as it was difficult to make the women repay in time. They also made pickles and sold it but marketing was a problem. Now the Group is not functioning. She says now she does not have enough time for it either. Sharmila has also worked with Smt. Anita Thapa, a B D C member, in an afforestation project in which trees were planted on 6 streets by 10 women who took care of the plants till they grew into big trees.

Sharmila's case shows that if a woman is motivated and has the support of her family she can achieve a lot. There are enough opportunities for rural women. What is needed is an increase in awareness and motivation and the will to take initiative and work hard.

**Rukmini Joshi**

Rukmini Joshi is a 45 year old courageous woman who lives in Mothrowala village. Her life is a saga of hard work, determination and perseverence. She has faced a number of problems and hardships in the last two decades but has emerged successful on the basis of her courage and help from some village elders. When she was quite young her husband deserted her with four small children to bring up. She has had only elementary education so she had to do any work, available, to feed her children. She said she has worked as a daily wage labourer, she has sold milk from house to house, she has worked in a bulb factory. She later bought a cycle to go to her work place and come back in the evening. She saw to it that her children got educated. She has two sons and two daughters. Now her eldest daughter is married, her older son is working as a mechanic, her younger daughter is doing graduation in MKP PG College and has also done a beautician's course and her youngest son is in high school. Some years back the Village Pradhan encouraged her to start a Self Help Group. She set up a group with 11 members and named it Prerna. She got a loan of Rs. 25,000 from the Government to run this SHG. The members were all poor rural women. They started a business of packing and selling pulses which they procured at wholesale rates. Besides they forwarded loans to members on a small interest rate. The group Prerna has its account at the Mini Bank at Jogiwala in which it has an amount of Rs. 16,000. The group provides all sorts of advice and also financial help to its members and other poor rural women.

Rukmini Joshi is highly respected by the villagers for her achievements. Today she has opened a shop for selling cement and takes care of it. She keeps in touch with the poor female daily-wage workers and tries to help them. She is consulted by the Pradhan in various important matters about the welfare of the village like construction of roads and other amenities. When the researcher planned to hold an awareness rally in Mothrowala, it was Rukmini Joshi who helped in organising it. She talked to the Pradhan, arranged for a location and motivated about 50 women and girls to attend the rally. She is a very confident and helpful person who is also very practical in her approach. She is interested in improving the lot of the women in her village. She plans to enter politics soon as many villagers are requesting her to contest the Panchayat elections. She says that a woman has to have the courage to achieve success and work hard for it. In bad times, generally no one helps, one has to fend for one's self. When her husband deserted her, her relatives did not come forward to help her. Now she does not expect any one to help her. She has taught her children also to help themselves. In fact, she personifies the saying, God helps those, who help themelves.

**Sarla Thapa**

Sarla Thapa is the Pradhan of the Village Panchayat of Swarn Jayanti Gram, Navada. She has won the election from a general seat and not a reserved seat, which shows that the villagers prefered her to other male contestants. Her term is from 2003 to 2008. The Panchayat in this village is very efficient and the researcher met the Secretary of the Panchayat at his office, who said that he came every week and mostly women came to get various jobs done. He said the women in Navada were very active in politics and had a high level of general awareness. The villagers are very happy with the work of Sarla Thapa and there are chances that she may be elected for another term. When interviewed, she said she is willing to serve the people once again. She is a middle aged woman with three children. Her son and elder daughter are married and the younger daughter has to be married. Her daughter-in-law stays at home. She has a big house and a Maruti car. Her husband does some business. She is an independent woman and takes her own decisions and works as the Pradhan on her own. Her priorities are providing basic facilities to the villagers. Navada is a developed village with most facilities like schools, health centre, Aanganwadi, Training programmes at the Panchayat, satisfactory water supply and electricity.

She said that 20 years back she had joined the Mahila Mangal Dal and started working for village welfare as its member. Then she was elected as its Vice President and finally as its President. She achieved a lot working in all these capacities, for instance as the President of the Dal, she decided that she should try to get electricity for a small village named Kumhar Basti. She started a struggle for this and met various officials and made many petitions. After some time she was successful in getting electric connections for the village. She says that she had promised the villagers that she would get electricity for them and so when she could fulfil her promise she felt great satisfaction. It gave her a new confidence to work for the betterment of the village and villagers. Next she started trying to get telephone connection for her village,

Navada. For this she struggled for three years; finally she was successful in getting phone connections for Navada. Presently she has applied for a loan of 20,000 for the village Panchayat. She has not yet received it but is busy trying for it. She says that she wants her village to prosper and improve still more. They have also started the Sarva Shiksha Abhiyan. She would like the women to get educated and trained so that they can earn and be economically independent. She says her work gives her great satisfaction, at the same time it has improved her standard of living. It has given her confidence and prestige. But it is also true that to achieve all this, she has worked very hard for more than two decades and faced many hurdles and difficulties.

**Kamala Jaiswal**

Kamala Jaiswal is a smart and efficient woman in her early forties. She is single and comes from a well to do family in Ajabpur. She says she has always been interested in doing social work. She feels driven to help her fellow beings specially women, to lead a good life with a decent standard of living. After her graduation she did some courses in public relations social work etc. and finally set up the Samarpit Sewa Sansthan in 1992. It is an NGO which is registered with the Government of India and works for rural uplift and women's empowerment. Its Head Office is in Ajabpur Kalan but it has branches in other Developmental Blocks of Dehradun district. The NGO is involved in various activities like running a Craft Centre for teaching women and girls tailoring and embroidery, holding health and awareness camps, organizing blood donation camps, helping farmers with rain water harvesting and testing quality of soil and water etc. It offers free courses of six month and one year duration to its students at the Craft center, which are recognized by ITI. This Centre gets aid from DRDA. In Sahaspur the NGO is running a rain water harvesting programme with the help of Watershed

Management Programme. In Ajabpur there is a Soil and Water analysis laboratory besides the craft center. Kamala Jaiswal supervises all this work. She has donated blood repeatedly at the camps. She has helped rural women to improve their lives by capacity building and becoming self-reliant. Her NGO has helped 69 women find gainful employment, to date and has helped in forming 27 SHGs in the villages. She is involved in motivating the villagers to maintain cleanliness and hygiene. She organised a Sampoorna Swachchata Abhiyan in the village to demand proper toilets for women. She has also participated in the Uttarakhand movement and was present at the Rampur Tiraha incident on 2nd October 2004. She is dedicated to her work and feels that she has still to do a lot for the rural women who are discriminated against and do not get sufficient access to basic facilities. Her NGO receives grants from the government for development work. Her work has been appreciated by the Governor of Uttaranchal. She is an example of a good leader and achiever.

**Hajira Begum**

Hajira Begum is a middle aged housewife living in Hansuwala. She has four children. Her husband is a well to do farmer. Hansuwala is a predominantly Muslim village. Hajira Begum has had primary education but her children, even her two daughters are well educated having done graduation from good colleges in Dehradun. In the last Panchayat elections, Hajira contested for the post of ward member from a reserved seat for women. She lost to a Sikh woman of the village. She said that she has no ill will or unpleasant feeling for having lost, because she feels the other person is more active and vocal. This shows her maturity of thought and her objectivity which is remarkable in a rural, little educated woman.

Generally Muslim women are confined to their homes, specially in the villages. With such a background, it is definitely a positive sign that Hajira contested the elections. This shows that Muslims, both men and women, have realized that they should join the mainstream and avail of all the opportunities that are offered. Secondly, providing higher education to daughters is also a very positive sign which will go a long way in empowering women. Hajira Begum is an ordinary housewife but she has shown that she has a progressive attitude and behaviour. This augurs well for her future and for that of her family. She has faced quite a few challenges in her life and accepted change when required. She said when she was newly married she lived with her in laws in a very conservative set up but with passage of time she started mixing with other women and joined the Mahila Mangal Dal. Her husband supported her in her activities. She has encouraged her daughters to study and does not differentiate between sons and daughters in spending for their needs. She has also joined a SHG to benefit from its activities. All this shows that she is interested in improving her life.

**Batulan**

Batulan is an old widow living in Mothrowala village. Her name suggests that she is a Muslim but she was married to a Scheduled caste man, Dinu who worked in the Railways as a sweeper. Now she lives with her sister-in-law Rani who is also a widow and her children. Her eldest daughter is also a widow and works in Dehradun. Batulan works in a couple of houses as a domestic help and also gets old age pension. But she says that she is not getting any pension from the railway although she has gone many times to the nearby railway station to petition her cause. She belongs to Saharanpur and since she married outside her community, she has no contacts with her own relatives. Now her in-laws and children are her only relations. In Mothrowala we find a lot of communal harmony and Hindus and Muslims live cheek by jowl. In Batulan's home too, her sister-in-law has always been like a sister to her, although she is a Hindu. Batulan has three children who are now all grown up. Her son is yet to get married. He is a casual labourer. There isn't enough money for him to get married. Batulan feels that in this world every one has to bear his own burden and no one helps the poor. Even the government schemes are mostly beneficial to the richer villagers. To some extent she is right, because most evaluations of rural development programmes have also noted this; but some efforts are on to help the poorest of the poor. For instance, she gets the old age pension of Rs.700 per six months, but she says it is too less and even from this meager amount the officials demand a commission. She does not know much about SHGs or other schemes for rural women. She believes in working hard to maintain her home and hearth. In spite of her bitterness and cynicism, she was friendly and cheerful during the conversation. She seems to be resigned to her fate which is an old characteristic of villagers. We can conclude that she is a gutsy woman although she is now too old to adopt new ways. She has self respect and works for her living. She wants to get what is due to her because it is her right. This itself is commendable in an illiterate old woman.

**Rajni**

Rajni is a young girl of 18 years. She lives in a small village in Jolly Grant with her family. They have a pucca house but are very poor. Her father is a casual labourer and her mother works as a sweeper in the Jolly Grant Hospital. They are four sisters and one brother. Rajni studied upto class VIII but now stays at home to do the housework. Her sisters and brother go to school. Rajni wants to do some vocational training but none is available free of cost, so she cannot afford it. She is about to be married soon, but she is quite apprehensive. Her parents cannot afford to give a dowry and she may be looked down upon or ill-treated by in-laws for this. She has no complain against her parents because they are doing all they can for the children. She is sad about not completing her schooling but it was just not possible, because when her mother got a job someone had to stay at home to work. She feels her parents have great expectations for their son and want him to study well and get a good job, but they do not neglect their daughters. They want to get their daughters married as soon as they can find good matches. This is the most practical approach and Rajni understands it. She says that after getting married if she gets a chance she will definitely learn some craft in order to become economically self-reliant. This shows that she is ambitious and given the opportunity will avail of it to improve her skills and empower herself. Her awareness has increased because she sees girls doing various vocational courses around her. Two girls of her village got the training for working in beauty parlour from Dehradun and are now working at a parlour near their village. This has inspired Rajni. There is every hope that in a few years Rajni too would be employed. She appears to be a vocal and determined person, who has learnt to adjust to realities very well.

**Janki Rawat**

Janki Rawat is a 50 years old woman who is very active and assertive. She had participated actively in the Uttarakhand Movement and was present among the agitators when the police forcibly stopped them at Rampur Tiraha on 2nd October 2004. She said that women were ill treated there and had to run into the sugarcane farms to hide from the police men. Some women were raped. Some young boys disappeared and were not found later. She says the Uttarakhand government has promised her a government job, but she has not got it yet. She said she was a member of the Mahila Mangal Dal and had worked for the welfare of village women for many years. Then she was involved in the Andolan for a separate state for nearly eight years. She has two grown up sons. One is employed. The other has just completed his education. Her husband leads a retired life. Even today, Janki is active in helping the villagers. She does not hold any public post but takes part in rallies and meetings organized by NGOs or Panchayat members for various social causes. She is a member of a Self Help Group which has just started functioning. The members plan to make pickles and papads and sell them. She is quite enthusiastic about this project. With her earlier experiences and her leadership qualities, she is bound to be successful. She is a satisfied housewife and does her household duties efficiently.

**Sunita Pal**

Sunita Pal is a young woman who is highly educated. She has done MA in Geography and is now doing her Ph.D under a Professor of DAV College. She belongs to Saharanpur. She got married to Gopal Singh Pal of Majri Grant some five years back. His family is quite rich and they are in the dairy business. They own a big house and many buffalos. Gopal and Sunita have started an English medium school in the village. In the beginning it was difficult for Sunita to adjust to village life but now she has got used to it, although in their family women do not tend to the cattle. There are servants to do this job. Sunita wants to complete her Ph.D soon and try for a lecturer's post in a college. She has the full support of her husband in her plans. Her husband is a graduate and he is capable of running the school. At present both are busy running the school efficiently. It is a primary school with 45 students and two teachers, besides them. It is recognized by the state government. They plan to develop the school into a high school in future. Sunita has two small children. The daughter is in KG and the son is two years old. Sunita manages her household duties, her school work and her Ph.D work very efficiently. She says she gets full support and help from her family members. Sunita is an example of an educated woman who has adjusted well to village life and is trying to make progress in her own situation. She is ambitious and hard working. There is every possibility of her achieving her goals, also because she has the full support of her family.

These case studies show the different levels of empowerment of women in the sample villages. Not all of them are big achievers, but they are all quite aware and ambitious, which is a very positive sign. Secondly all of them are satisfied with their life situations and are trying to do their best to improve in the existing circumstances. Adjustment and compromise are essential qualities for women to achieve their objectives. Of course hard work and dedication are also necessary, but confrontation is not advisable, as it creates more problems. These case studies show us that, rural women, be they educated or not, are quite practical and worldly wise and handle their circumstances with patience and finesse. They know their limitations and are trying to do the best they can in existing conditions. With some motivation and help from government or non-government agency they would be able to realize their full potential and improve their lives.

# Bibliography


1. Arunachalam Jaya Women' Equality-A Struggle for Survival, 2005, Gyan Publishing House New Delhi.
2. Arya Sadhana Women, Gender Equality and the State, 2000, Deep and Deep Publications.
3. Agarwal Beena Who Sows, Who Reaps-Women and Land Rights in India, 1988 Journal of Peasant India.
4. Anjum Mohini Muslim Women in India, 1992, Radiant Publishers
5. Bhattacharya Malini Globalization, 2004, Tulika Books.
6. Bahuguna Anjali [Ed] Science and Technology in relation to Rural Women, 1990, Har Anand Publication.
7. Bose Ashish Empowerment through Capacity Building, 2004, Samskriti.
8. Bhose Joel SGR NGOs and Rural Development, 2003, Concept Publishing Company.
9. Burra, Ranadive, Murthy Micro Credit, Poverty and Empowerment, Linking the Triad [Ed] 2005 Sage Publications.
10. Balakrishnan A Rural Landless Women Labourers, 2005 Kalpaz Publications.
11. Banu Zenab Disempowerment of Tribal Women-Perspectives on 73rd Constitutional Amendment, 2004 Kanishka Publishers Delhi.

12. Basu Rasil Women and Governance–Re-imagining the State, 2003, Ektara New Delhi.
13. Buxmusa & Gupte Assistance for Women's Development-Housing, 1992 Popular Prakashan Bombay.
14. Clayton, Dent & Dubois Rural Planning in Developing Countries, 2003, Earth Scan India.
15. Crowell Daniel W The SEWA Movement and Rural Development, 2001 Sage Publications.
16. Chaturvedi Pradeep Women and Food Security-Role of Panchayats [Ed] 2002 Concept Publishing Company.
17. Dhar S N Micro Finance for Women, 2004, Northern Book Centre.
18. Dutta R K Women Empowerment, 2000, Reference Press.
19. Giriappa S Role of Women in Rural Development, 1988, Daya Publishing House.
20. Goel Aruna Education and Socio-Economic Perspectives of Women, 2005, Development and Empowerment, Deep and Deep Publications.
21. Jassal Smita Tiwari Daughters of the Earth, 2001, Manohar.
22. Jhabvala, Sudarshan, Unni Informal Economy Centre-stage [Eds] 2003 Sage Publications.
23. Joshi MV Women Rural Labourers, 1999.
24. Karat Brinda Survival and Emancipation 2006, Three Essays.
25. Kandari & Gosain Garhwal Himalaya 2001 Trans Media Shrinagar.
26. Khan Saigol & Zia Aspects of Women and Development, 1995 ASR Publications.
27. Krishna Sumi Livelihood and Gender [Ed] 2003 Sage Publications.

28. Kumar Hajira & Varghese Women's Empowerment-Issues, Challenges and Strategies 2004 Regency Publications.

29. Kumar Ashok Women and Development 2002 A P H Publications.

30. Kapadia Karen Women and Work 1988 Encyclopaedia of Women' s Studies Vol. 2.

31. Krishnaraj M & Desai N Women and Society in India 1987 Ajanta Books International.

32. Laxmi Devi A Rural Women 1987 Northern Book Centre. New Delhi.

33. Manuja Devi K Rural Women-Poverty Alleviation Programme 1997 Anmol Publications. New Delhi.

34. Mondal Sekh Rahim Rural Muslim Women 2005 Northern Book Centre. New Delhi.

35. Mill John Stuart [1996 edition] Subjection of Women [Eds] Mukherji & Ramaswamy Deep and Deep Publications.

36. Murty & Gaur Women Work Participation and Empowerment 2002 RBSA Publications Jaipur.

37. Murty S Women and Employment 2001 RBSA Publications Jaipur.

38. Mukherjee & Bhattacharya Conditioning and Empowerment of Women [Eds] 2003 Gyan Publishing House New Delhi.

39. Narasimhan S Empowering Women 1999 Sage Publications.

40. Neerja K P Rural Women 2000 Discovery Publishing House.

41. Puthenkalam John Joseph Empowerment-Sustainable Human Development Strategy for Poverty Alleviation 2004 Rawat Publications, Jaipur & Delhi.

42. Rao A [Ed.] Gender and Caste 2002 Kali for Women.

43. Rahman Zainab Women and Society 2005 Kalpaz Publications New Delhi.

44. Saksena Kiran Women and Politics [Ed] 2000 Gyan Publishing House.

45. Saran & Sandhwar Problem of Women Worker in Unorganised Sector 1990 Northern Book Centre New Delhi.

46. Sinha A K Panchayati Raj and Empowerment of Women 2003 Northern Book Centre New Delhi.

47. Scott Catherine V. Gender and Development 1993 Lynne Rienner Publishers Boulder London.

48. Singh S N Muslims in India 2003 Anmol Publications.

49 Singh AK Empowerment of Women in India 2000 Publications.

50. Singh, Bakshi, Rathore et al Economic Empowerment of Rural Women in India [Eds.] 2003 RBSA Publishers.

51. Samanta R K [Ed.] Empowering Rural Women-Issues, Opportunities & Approaches 2004 The Women Press. Delhi.

52. Grover Indu & Grover Deepak Empowerment of Women 2002 Geeta Somani Agrotech Publishing Academy Udaipur.

53. Shiva Vandana Staying Alive-Women, Ecology and Development 1987 Kali for Women.

54. Tapan Neeta Need for Women's Empowerment 1998, Rawat Publications.

55. Verma & Nath Women and Rural Development Programmes 2005 B R Publishing Corporation.

56. Wigma Raja Ponna Women Poverty and Resources 1989 Sage Publications.

57. Sudesh Arya Parvateeya Nari, Sangharsh Gaatha 2004 Uttarakhand Computer Graphics Haridwar.

58. Unniyal Ekta The Study of Uttaranchal, 2003, Mentor Publications Dehradun.

### *Newspapers and Journals*

1. TheTimes of India New Delhi.
2. Economic and Political Weekly Mumbai.
3. The Eastern Anthropologist-Ethnographic and Folk Culture Society, Lucknow. Published by Serial Publications New Delhi.
4. Manushi New Delhi.

### *Resource Material of Women's Study Centres*

1. Course Material of International Training Programme on Poverty and Livelihood Options for Rural Women. Centre for Gender Studies. National Institute of Rural Development. Rajendranagar Hyderabad AP.
2. Proceedings of 4th and 6th Referesher Courses in Women's Studies. Centre for Women's Studies and Development. BHU Varanasi UP.

### *Government of India Publications*

1. Towards Equality-The Unfinished Agenda. Working Group on Empowerment of Women-Tenth Plan [M o HRD] Published by National Commission for Women [2002] .
2. Platform.for Action. India Country Report Published by Ministry of HRD Govt. of India

### *Government of Uttaranchal Publications*

1. Asha-Swashakti Pariyojna Uttaranchal Published by Department of Women's Empowerment and Child Development. Government of Uttaranchal.
2. Annual Report of Completion of Projects 2004-2005 Published by Department of Women's Empowerment and Child Development Government of Uttaranchal.

### *Report of NGOs*

Annual Reports of Samarpit Sewa Sansthan 2004–05 and 2005-06.

Published by Samarpit Ajabpur.

Brochures of NGOs, Women's Study Centres and Govt. Deptts.

1. Brochure of Centre for Gender Studies, NIRD Hyderabad.
2. Brochure of Disha, Sahaspur.

Brochure of Department of Women's Empowerment and Child Development Government of Uttaranchal.

# Index

G



H



I